live wires

live wires

Powerful stories of changed lives

D.J. Carswell

Authentic

16 15 14 13 12 11 10 8 7 6 5 4 3 2

First published 2007 by Authentic Media
Reprinted 2010 by Authentic Media Limited
Milton Keynes
www.authenticmedia.co.uk

British Library Cataloguing in Publication Data
A catalogue record for this book is available from the British Library

ISBN 978-1-85078-737-2

Names have been changed in Chapter 15 to protect identities

Cover Design by Dan Collins
Printed and bound in Great Britain by J.F. Print, Sparkford

Dedication

In gratitude to my mother, Evelyn Hill, who taught me to love words and literature, and gave me something she herself would have enjoyed . . . a good education.

Contents

Acknowledgements

I am grateful to all who have contributed to this book, especially those who have shared their stories with me. Many thanks to my editor, Emma Newrick, to Rhoda Carswell for proof reading and to the team at Authentic Media. Special thanks go to my husband Roger, my real 'live wire', and our children, Emma, Ben, Hannah and Jonathan, for their various contributions and encouragement.

Introduction

Many of us have had an electric shock. We never expect it, of course . . . a powerful encounter that takes us by surprise. Life sometimes throws us together with individuals whose lives have something special about them. A zest, a *je ne sais quoi*, sets them apart with a power that rarely leaves our own lives unmarked. People are fascinating, and the bunch you will meet in the following pages are a real mixture from all walks of life, cultures and ages. What they have in common is an encounter with someone who was to change their lives . . . for the better. Maybe you will meet Him too and if you do, let me know!

CHAPTER ONE

The Barman

It is said that you can tell a man by his friends. Graham's were thieves, prostitutes and murderers. His job as a barman took him into some of the seediest bars in Toronto, Canada. But it was all a far cry from the respectable start in life back home in Essex, England.

When Graham was a teenager all the talk was of war. Whole families were to experience tremendous upheavals, changes and losses. Faith, if you had any, was severely tested in many cases. Graham's own commitment to God was sidelined as, in the company of other lads his age, he joined the Merchant Navy. It was only a matter of time before he adopted the dubious lifestyle of the stereotypical 'drunken sailor'. Alcohol is a powerful drug that is peddled throughout society with a sense of respectability that it does not deserve. Graham found that the alcohol gave him confidence among his peers and broke down his inhibitions. At each port of call, drink and women were available to the men. 'Every time I fell to temptation

I found my conscience got harder,' Graham recalls. 'Out in the Middle East I saw more evil, sex and vice than one could imagine existed, but I never "blinked an eye".'

Graham's life, like the lives of many of the lads his age, was descending into an abyss of vice and depravity from which he would struggle to escape. Surrounded by his mates, it was easy to be sucked into bad ways and habits that he once might have shunned. With the end of the war came the shock and shame of having to return to his home. It is to his credit that he did in fact still have some respect for his family's feelings and was conscious of feeling shame at his behaviour. But there was no remorse or change of behaviour . . . instead he decided to get away from home and head for London.

One day, half-drunk, he walked into the emigration office in Piccadilly Circus and requested to go to Canada! Forms were pushed under his nose. No one spotted his deliberate lie as he described his occupation as 'farmer'. The medical officer who performed the mandatory medical confirmed that Graham was 'breathing'. And that was that! He was free to depart for Toronto the following week.

Of course, the young 'farmer' was immediately taken to the specially designated farms in his new adopted country. But a few of the lads got together and thought, 'Nobody is holding us, so why don't we go?' So they picked up their bags and walked out. Together they managed to book into a cheap hotel, but they still had to find work. Eventually Graham managed to secure employment with the Canadian National Railway, as a waiter in the dining cars. 'This was on the long-distance train from Winnipeg to Chicago. I don't think we were ever sober.'

The strange thing is that Graham still thought of himself as respectable . . . even though he drank a lot, for he was young and considered he 'could take it'. Completely taken in by this delusion, he couldn't foresee the impending dangers when he changed jobs and began working in downtown bars, which were some of the seediest you can imagine. His friends were now blasphemers, thieves, prostitutes and murderers. Experience has taught Graham that once you get sucked into this way of life, you find you can't live with respectable people.

His friends were now blasphemers, thieves, prostitutes and murderers.

One of the bars he worked in was a place where every crook imaginable would hang out. It was in an area where a person couldn't walk the streets at night or they would be mugged. On his way to work at night, sometimes a shadowy figure would come out of an alleyway and Graham would hear someone say, 'That's Graham the bartender,' and they would slip back into the ominously dark shadows again. By now he had become part of the scene. As a 'regular' he was constantly being questioned by the police.

'If there was a big robbery the night before, the next day there wouldn't be a crook in sight, but more policemen.

'"Who was in here yesterday?"

'"I don't know. I didn't notice."

'Of course the cops knew you were lying; and a few days later whoever had made the "big haul" would slip you a $50 or $100 tip for keeping quiet.'

The scariest time Graham ever had was when a fellow called Skip was shot down by the police as he was climbing in a window. Two afternoons later Graham was in the bar when this same man, Skip, walked in! 'It's Skippy!' he cried out. 'But you're dead!'

He genuinely thought he had seen a ghost, but in fact it was Skip's brother. He walked up to Graham at the bar, displayed two guns inside his coat and said, 'I am going to ask you just once, and if you don't give me the right answer . . . you're dead. Who was Skippy drinking with?'

Graham tried to think – he didn't want to make a mistake! Just at that moment, the owner poked his head around the door, was across the room in no time and after whispering in the man's ear, led him to the office. It was, without a doubt, a timely intervention for it turned out that the man was insane. Some time later he was arrested in Chicago and went to the electric chair.

You might have thought that this was an isolated occasion, but it wasn't. Working in the bar was extremely dangerous. One night a one-armed man came in shouting, 'I am going to kill somebody tonight.' Everyone dived for cover as bullets and glass flew all over the place. Within two minutes there were squad cars, sirens and gunfire . . . just like in a movie.

'People think those films are an exaggeration, but they're not,' comments Graham. 'Life is truly like that in some places, yet you can be living in the same city and have no idea that such violence is there, other than what you read in the newspaper.'

Graham was no longer an innocent youth with ambition. The man he had become was 'hard-bitten' and tough . . . tough enough to keep a baseball bat behind the bar in order to defend himself. He was a tough, drunken, thieving, gambling character just like his friends, by his own admission. He had reached rock bottom.

Graham knew he needed to change. He still felt a strong pull to the sea, so he signed on for work on the cargo ships that plied the Great Lakes. Unfortunately, he didn't stop drinking. But eventually he gained some common sense from somewhere, making him think about straightening his life out and giving him the desire to go home and see his family.

The trip back to England was successful in that he did manage to reform himself somewhat. He also found a wife. After his marriage he returned to Canada with Kay. Any hopes he had of continuing his personal reform didn't last though, for not long after, he began drinking and gambling more and more. Despite going back to working behind the bar, Graham did at least choose respectable places to work this time.

New Year's Resolution

Sometimes, when you least expect it, something happens that will forever be etched on your memory.

Graham was doing what he always did at that time on New Year's Eve . . . he was celebrating with a drink. This particular year he was sipping whisky from the bottle when midnight struck. The television was on, flickering in the corner. Graham remembers it as if it were yesterday.

'All of a sudden this beautiful choir came on to the TV singing hymns. Then suddenly it was as though I was transported back into my childhood. Memories came flooding back. But there before me still was my present God-forsaken life. The music completely broke me and I, the hard man, wept many tears. I must have sat there all night long with this strange "warmth" within me. Then the dreadful realization of my wrongdoing, my sin, came to me. What had I done?'

It was his personal day of reckoning . . . his soul laid bare and found wanting. With the morning light and the promise of the first day of the new year, Kay suggested that perhaps Graham should go to church again. Was God doing something in her heart too?

'God's rehabilitation process in my life has been very slow, sometimes tender and sometimes chastening. At times I have stumbled along the way, but gradually many of the evils have fallen away. When I suffered a heart attack, I remember saying to the Lord, "O God, I can't meet you now . . . I'm not ready." You see, I still had no assurance that God had accepted me and forgiven me. I felt no inner joy and peace. I lacked true Christian joy because I continued to look back and mourn over my lost years.'

By now Graham and his wife were attending a church in Pontefract, in the north of England. At one of the special services held there each year, entitled 'Faith for Our Times', the speaker was Paul Bassett. One of the verses quoted from the Bible that evening was 'I will heal their waywardness and love them freely' (Hos. 14:4).

Graham realized when he heard those words that God had indeed healed and forgiven him for going away from Him. True joy and peace were his from then on.

'The scars of my past life will not be completely erased from my memory, but how wonderful that God chooses *not* to remember. This understanding of God's boundless love brought a peace that has lasted to this day. I am not ashamed of the gospel because it is the power of God for the salvation of everyone who believes. I know now that nobody is too bad for God to be able to change them.'

CHAPTER TWO

The Patient

'Girls of twelve don't get cancer – surely they don't. I've never heard of anyone my age getting it. It's what old people get, isn't it?'

Her wide brown eyes roamed round the occupants of ward E29. A small figure lay asleep amid drip stands bleeping every five minutes. Some parents were watching television. The visiting posse of doctors and nurses gathered around another bed. Someone down the corridor cracked a joke, which sparked off infectious, stifled giggles. The arrival of the drinks trolley brought light relief to the tedium of ward rounds, drug rounds, cleaning rounds . . .

Round and round Rachel's thoughts raced.

In a cheerful mood, one week ago, she had entered this strange world of groans and expressionless faces. 'Poor children,' she had thought to herself. 'They are really poorly.' Not for a single moment did it cross her mind that she herself had a serious illness too. Last year her spine had developed a curve. After several tests Rachel thought she was finally going to get it sorted out.

There was always something happening at Rachel's home. Be it little sister Naomi roller-blading in the garden with her friends, or older brothers Steve and Dave and their friends with their endless music and computer games, the house was never empty. Rachel's passion was ballet. Not content with just lessons on Saturdays, she enjoyed ballet music all week, besides entertaining herself and friends with dances she choreographed. Beautiful floaty scraps of fabric were fashioned into dance dresses by tying them round her waist. Graceful movements and poise are so important to a dancer, as is noticing every detail – including that shoulder, so straight normally, which now appeared to slope.

'Then there was all the school stuff . . . I didn't find school easy but I liked being there. I just wanted to get my back sorted out so that I could get on with life.'

The consultant at the hospital must have dreaded the day when he finally had to give Rachel the results of her tests. He gently and caringly explained that the curves, which had so quickly appeared in her spine, were caused by tumours around her brain and the length of her spine. Rachel had never heard of tumours so was not unduly worried. A biopsy was needed to find out if the tumours were growing slowly or quickly. This would enable him to make a decision about how to treat them. Not until the tumours were sorted out could an operation to straighten the spine be considered. 'OK,' she thought, 'that's a nuisance – two operations instead of one, but let's get it out of the way.'

The truth that children do indeed suffer from cancer could not be hidden and Rachel's head began to spin in disbelief. Yet as she looked around the ward, the truth was slowly sinking in.

'Children do get cancer. Some of them were younger than me.'

It finally hit her that this business of her spine wasn't going to be a straightforward job. The treatment to get rid of the tumours was to last a whole year. 'I was likely to feel sick for a large chunk of that time, but that wasn't the worst. I would lose my hair – all of it! I bent my head, shaking my long hair out in front of me. Sadly, I pulled at a lock of my dark brown hair, holding it against my thigh. Optimism drained away quite suddenly. I could put up with everything else but surely I didn't have to lose my hair. But there was no mistake. It was the future I had to face, but I wasn't ready for it. For the first time in hospital, I cried and cried . . . into my pillow . . . into my mum's arms . . . to God . . . to anyone who would listen. My sadness was overwhelming.'

In the relative quietness of the ward that night, as the staff talked in stage whispers and wheeled in new patients, Rachel lay thinking. Her tears had subsided. 'I needed a plan.' At only twelve, a year seemed a lifetime. She couldn't think of a single pastime, good or bad, that had lasted so long. 'I imagined it as a mountain. It would be long and hard, but I would reach the top in the end. I saw myself struggling uphill step by step. The thought was comforting.'

'God, please help me climb this mountain,' Rachel whispered. She felt calmer and drifted off into a peaceful sleep.

Andrew Lloyd Webber's musical, *Starlight Express*, was on at a theatre in London. Rachel's parents decided she should have a treat before she started chemotherapy. 'It was amazing . . . so fast, colourful and such fun that I forgot my turmoil as I immersed myself in the whirl of light and music. "There's a light at the end of the tunnel," the final song blasted out, "the inside might be as black as the night but at the end of the tunnel there's a light." It made me think that somehow I'd get through.'

Chemotherapy

'The plastic tubing that joined me to the bag hanging on my drip stand felt like a chain. I felt dirty . . . it was like I was fighting a bad mood all the time. Something unknown, unwanted was being pumped into my bloodstream. A much younger child, also on chemo-therapy, scooted up and down the ward on her drip stand. I giggled to myself while also feeling ashamed of being so miserable.'

Chemo was all it promised to be and worse. Rachel was nauseous so she couldn't eat. (Lots of people kindly sent her money 'for chocolate to cheer you up'. As she couldn't face chocolate, she bought lights from the Gadget Shop!) The family tried to do something positive each day, even if it was just having a friend round or going to Asda. 'I kept thinking, "I'll have a big party with my friends at the end of all this."

'I was sick. I didn't want to eat. I just wanted to sleep to escape this awful feeling, but waves of nausea penetrated my subconscious so that I never felt fully rested. My hair, which was now cut to shoulder length, became thinner and thinner. Eventually it fell out altogether.' Three months of this made her feel very weary, but then something alarming began to happen. She felt unsteady on her feet. One day, as she was walking into a crowded restaurant with her parents, she just fell over. The incident unnerved Rachel. She couldn't explain why it had happened and everyone was looking at her. 'I felt clumsy and stupid. They didn't tell me the treatment would do this. It scared me. I was thirteen by now. A teenager with a bald head.'

The bad news was that the chemotherapy was not working so would have to be stopped. But it wasn't the treatment that was making her fall over ... it was the tumours. 'I suppose I should have been scared that the treatment wasn't working, but my overwhelming feeling was one of relief that I could stop the chemotherapy.' The tumours were growing, thus interfering with her ability to walk. She was issued with crutches, but not long after had to use a wheelchair. Rachel experienced the embarrassment of having to be pushed everywhere, but there was no alternative. Suddenly her view of life was vertically challenged. She saw everything from a different level and her independence disappeared. She was a dancer confined to a chair. Rachel found that it was painfully slow to walk, especially as she was afraid of falling over all the time. Back home, Mum and Dad moved her bed downstairs because it was such a struggle for her to climb the stairs.

> I felt clumsy and stupid. They didn't tell me the treatment would do this. It scared me. I was thirteen by now. A teenager with a bald head.

Radiotherapy

It was like playing catch-up all the time as events in her life began to take over.

Once more, the family's daily routine was readjusted to fit in with Rachel's new treatment schedule. On the one hand, radiotherapy was not as bad as the chemo, but on the other hand, it was more stressful and time-consuming for all the family.

One major difference was that Rachel had to attend Nottingham City Hospital every day. By the time she had gone through the painfully slow routine of getting out of bed, bathing, dressing and generally doing what all teenage girls do, with Mum's help, she was ready to face the world and the twenty-mile journey by car.

As the front door clicked shut behind her Rachel knew that a new experience was awaiting her in the few hours ahead. The medical team had prepared her and supported the family by carefully explaining what was going to happen. Nevertheless, it must have been very daunting as she left home wondering how she would cope.

Rachel was not alone in the car. Dad and Mum took turns driving. But a few famous celebrities who made the journey so much more inviting, also accompanied them. Harry Potter was a great friend. Rachel never tired of hearing about his amazing adventures with Ron and Hermione. Even Captain Mainwaring and the lads of *Dad's Army* squeezed in somehow beside the magic wardrobe that was the entrance to C.S. Lewis's Narnia. Yes, audiotapes were definitely a distraction from fearful thoughts and traffic jams.

The first hurdle to overcome was the waiting room. As the door swung open, Rachel felt all eyes on her. Who would be next? The sound of people leafing through dog-eared celebrity magazines contributes to the tedium of waiting until someone breaks the silence and suddenly conversations break out, confidences, jokes and general chit-chat are shared – unless the television is on.

Rachel made many friends over the days and weeks she spent waiting for her treatments. Mostly older people, they took to this young girl who was going through the same things as they were.

'They became my friends. I used to enjoy doing embroidery, which the ladies would always come over and look at and admire. My long painted nails, which I was very proud of, were also a point of interest with them. We would exchange horror stories about our hospital experiences and console each other. Mum said we shouldn't because we would scare each other, but she didn't understand. It was what we had in common. It was what we were.'

When at last the dreaded moment came, Rachel was wheeled into the treatment room to have a body mask made for her to lie on. No one was allowed in while radiotherapy was being administered.

'The back of my head was clamped into a mould and I would wait while everyone left me alone. My heart beat faster as I held my breath waiting for the small bleeping sound, which would herald the arrival of a strange smell. A *very* strange smell.' Actually, it was so nasty that Rachel couldn't help worrying that it might damage her health! 'I know that was stupid really, because they were trying to save me.' Then everything would be over and she was free until the same time the next day. It left her in a weakened state with the feeling of nausea. Incredibly, Rachel was still managing to stay cheerful. Over many hours she amused and busied herself with her Game Boy, sewing, silk painting and making friendship bracelets for her friends.

Where did school feature in all of this? When she first began chemotherapy she had tried to continue with school whenever there was a break between treatments, but after a while it just became too much for Rachel. 'I felt tired and ill all the time. I wanted to be there, but if I went, I would end up having to be brought home again. Once I started radiotherapy, I didn't even try. I was exhausted.'

Despite all the problems, there was a ray of hope. Successive scans showed that the tumours had reduced somewhat. 'I could look forward to rebuilding my life. It was a great feeling.'

Yet only days after receiving the good news, she began to experience neck pains.

'At first I pushed it from my mind, strengthened by the positive scan pictures, but it refused to be ignored. Painkillers didn't seem to make any difference.'

Actually, Rachel's condition was a cause for concern as her already meagre appetite was diminishing rapidly. Her dramatic weight loss was so apparent that her family feared to see how skinny she was getting. Everyone tried to persuade her to eat, to no avail.

Christmas and New Year

The festive season was bursting with the usual excesses of a material world. Seasonal smells of roast turkey, stuffing and Christmas pudding pervaded every home. Everywhere people rushed about, dashing into shops to buy those last-minute gifts for family and friends. Despite the limitations of Rachel's condition, her family tried to make the most of the opportunity Christmas provided to enjoy family time and celebrate the spirit of giving. They brought out all the old family board games and everyone congregated in her room, which was lit up with fun and laughter.

'For me, the year 2000 brought a very special Christmas. I couldn't join in because I was confined to my bed, so it all came to me instead. Family and friends sat by my bed, shared gifts and played games. But I couldn't eat and I was in pain. It hurt to be hugged.'

All too soon, it seemed, the decorations were taken down and the cards collected, leaving the rooms looking bare. A new year had arrived . . . what would it bring? Resolutions were made with high hopes of better things for the future. For Rachel there was the prospect of more scans which would help the doctors answer her questions: Why am I in pain? Why don't I have any appetite?

The devastating news came at last. 'The tumours had grown in different places around the spine and brain. This time there was no cure. So I would die, I guessed.

'It was a time of crisis. Who should I speak to? There was my mum, who is great, but I am a teenager and you don't necessarily want to pour your heart out to your mum. I wondered who to call. I was really privileged to have lots of fantastic friends who had said that I could call them at any time . . . but this was mid-morning. Most of them would be at school or work. Then I remembered that my friend John would be at home. He was a retired gentleman, very friendly with a round face and short white beard that made him look a bit like Captain Birdseye in the fish adverts on television. He used to be a sailor as well! I asked my mum to call him and he came straight round.'

Rachel told him everything while she was crying and shaking with fear. She poured out her heart until he interrupted.

'Hey, stop it,' he said. 'What are you afraid of? What if you *do* die?'

Rachel knew then for certain that she had picked the right person. She breathed deeply as she sought to bring her emotions under control.

'John wasn't in a hurry for my answer,' she remembers. 'I thought quietly to myself. I was afraid of pain. I had had enough of that already, but I had no need to be afraid of dying, had I? I thought back to the Kids' Club that I went to at church where a hundred children played games every Friday night and learned about the Bible. I thought back to when I first understood that Jesus, God's Son, had died in my place. Even at that young age I knew I did and thought wrong things sometimes. I thought it incredible that God could love us all so much when mostly we take no notice of Him. I remembered going home and quietly praying to God in my room. I thanked Him that Jesus had taken my punishment and I asked Him to make me His child. Since that day, I'd been certain that God was with me whether things were going well or badly.

'I knew if I died, God would give me life forever.

'I looked up at John. "I'll go to heaven," I said.

'"Are you afraid of going to heaven?" he enquired.

'"No, I'm not." I was beginning to feel surer of myself. "No, it will be good to see Jesus, but I am afraid of pain and, well, it doesn't seem right. Not yet . . . I am only thirteen."

> As we prayed together there in my bedroom I knew I could face the future again with God's help.

'"Look Rachel, we're going to keep on praying that God will make you better. You don't need to plan on dying. But we will all die one day. So long as we know we are ready to meet God, we don't have to keep worrying about it. We can live life to the full."

'I knew John was right. As we prayed together there in my bedroom, I knew I could face the future again with God's help.'

'Don't worry,' she told her parents later that day, 'I'm not worried. Don't be sad. Don't let Steve, Dave and Naomi [her brothers and sister] be sad either.'

'My mum and dad smiled,' she recalls, 'but their eyes were filled with tears. I had already dried mine. I was ready to move on.

'"You can tell the relatives and friends how things are," I told them, "but I don't want to keep talking about it." What was the point? I wanted to think about trying to get well. I'd rather have a laugh with my friends, enjoy a good film or read a book.'

Changes

Rachel's condition was now quite obviously a cause for concern. Her doctors suggested that she should try a mild chemotherapy drug. It was to be taken for two weeks followed by three weeks off. Maybe it would hold off the tumours for a short while. Rachel agreed.

'I will try anything!' she told the medical staff. This time the drug was not administered by intravenous drip, but orally.

'Yuk! It tasted like you would expect cleaning fluid to taste!' she exclaimed. 'However, the good thing was that it meant I wouldn't have to keep going to hospital. Hooray!'

Actually, Rachel liked the people at Queens Medical. The doctors and nurses were all very friendly and approachable, but she couldn't help worrying that someone was going to come and stick a needle in her or give her something nasty to drink. She was determined though, come what may, that she would stay out of hospital.

One thing that was painfully obvious to all and needed to be sorted out was the issue of her weight.

'I looked like a famine victim,' Rachel recalls wistfully, 'but I couldn't force myself to eat. I felt sick whenever I tried. I finally agreed to be fed through a tube, which passed into my nose, down the back of my throat and into my stomach. Morphine soon took care of the pain.'

Now that it appeared that Rachel's activities were limited very much to the confines of her home (especially as her condition did not look like improving), the family and social services combined their efforts to make her life as comfortable as possible. A stair lift was fitted and even a bath lift. She was given an electronic easy chair – the type elderly people use to help them stand up. 'I was grateful for the help – I needed it so much, but I couldn't help feeling a bit useless. I had hoped to return to school, but there was no way, for I was much too weak.'

Educational stimulus, however, was not considered impossible. Despite her weakened condition, Rachel's mind was still active and her spirit strong. If she could not make it to school, then school would have to come to her. It came in the form of Susan, her own personal tutor. 'I wasn't all that keen on the idea at first, but I shouldn't have worried. Susan soon became more like a friend than a teacher, helping me tackle subjects a little at a time. We even did cookery – in the lounge! We did our best to get the flour off the easy chairs before my mum came in.'

The gastric tube method of feeding slowly began to pay off. She looked forward to trips out in the wheelchair, even if there could be a downside to them. Kids, being what they are, never fake their emotions so when Rachel was in shops it was not uncommon for kids to stare at her. 'I suppose I couldn't blame them really. I bet they had never seen a girl with no hair and a tube stuck up her nose. If I was feeling low, I struggled with the attention. I'd look away and shed a few tears. Mostly though, I'd stare back or smile widely and wave. If they were more than five or six years old they'd look away embarrassed to be caught gawping. I enjoyed having the last laugh!'

So the days passed into months, with cycles of chemotherapy and . . . treats. Sometimes there would be a visit to Rainbows, the children's hospice that she was growing to love as her visits increased. Sometimes there would be a trip to a show – *Disney on Ice, Riverdance* or the circus. It made all the difference to Rachel if she had something to look forward to during treatment. Kind friends were always coming up with something. The charity When You Wish Upon a Star even took her to Lapland for a day, with other poorly children, at Christmas.[1]

Facing the Future

Instead of Rachel's condition slowly becoming worse, as was expected by her medical team, to their delight she became gradually stronger. One day she was asked if she would like to go back to school, just in small doses. Can you imagine going back into the classroom with no hair? True, it was beginning to grow a little, but it was hardly looking 'normal' yet.

'I knew my friends wouldn't laugh, but there was everyone else and I felt too weak to stand up for myself. The thing that changed my mind was helping out at the church Kids' Club. They get about a hundred children who do crafts, games and other activities. I wanted to help but didn't think I could. Then, on a sudden urge, I offered to teach some of them to sing in a group. Each day I enjoyed myself so much, especially as the kids didn't laugh at me or make faces. I got my confidence back and decided to go back to school after a gap of almost three years!'

The chemotherapy finally came to an end, as did the need for morphine. The nasal gastric tube was out and

Rachel was eating respectable-sized meals ('Well, almost!' she admits with a grin). The tumours, however, remain.

'At church we used to sing a song based on something God said in the Bible: I "will never leave you nor forsake you" (Deut. 31:6). It stuck in my mind when I was struggling so much and it is what makes me more confident about the future – whatever it might bring. I know that when I die I will be with God, not because I am good or religious, but because I have asked Jesus to take away all my sin. He rose from the dead and has given me life with Him right now, through death and forever in heaven. There will be no tears or pain there.'

Update

'Well, a lot has happened. The year I went back to school I managed to get a GCSE in childcare. I know it's only one – but it meant a lot to me after having missed so many lessons. At the school awards night, imagine my surprise when I was presented with the Princess Diana Memorial Award for Achieving Against the Odds!

'Since then I have had my spine straightened. The procedure took three operations and many weeks. I wondered if I had done the right thing when I was in the middle of it, but I am so glad I did now. I look and feel so much better.

I am now at college studying Art and Design. I gave up the idea of childcare since I am not steady on my feet. I have always enjoyed art and I hope to become a costume designer. I have always loved designing dance outfits. After all, if I can't wear them myself, I might as well make them for people who can!'

CHAPTER THREE

The Page Three Photographer

The camera's eye
Does not lie,
But it cannot show
The life within.

W.H. Auden, 'Runner'

Ken's ambition had *not* been to be a Page Three photographer, but that's what he became. It was all a far cry from the early days of his youth in the Leicester Choral Society and Boys Brigade. At the age of eighteen he signed up for the RAF, serving in Malaysia. The boy became a man. Barrack rooms are an education in themselves. If you survive life there you can probably cope anywhere. Discipline had to be learned; courage and bravery were expected. It was a tough life, but not without compensations. He made some good mates and travelled to parts of the world he would otherwise not have gone to. Leaving behind the steamy climate of the Far East, he suffered culture shock on his return to Leicester.

Many of the men, including Ken, had girlfriends waiting for them. Olive and Ken made their vows in church and settled down to married life with all its hopes and expectations. Their first child was a girl . . . and the second . . . and the third. Job prospects seemed quite good in one place as a sports officer, but there were problems that upset him, so nothing came of it.

The family moved down to Bournemouth on the south coast. An unsettled period followed with Ken again being upset by people's behaviour. One man he met would one moment swear in conversation and the next be in church praying. It put him off church. Later on in life he understood that, in England, not all people who say they are Christians all mean the same thing or correspond to the biblical definition. It didn't worry him that much, though, as he had plenty of other things to occupy his mind.

A regular income was needed for Ken's fast-growing family. Work with a photographic firm was going to give him some opportunities, but a job at a finance company also helped things along. The blokes that he worked with must have envied him, as in his spare time he covered things such as beauty contests. At one such event he met a girl who came third, but later went on to become a Miss World. Close links developed between her and the family. By 1971 Ken was working part-time and evenings taking photos of both a Miss UK and a Miss World. Being close to the beach enabled him to get good shots that would be excellent to sell to newspapers. He hoped that they would be money-spinners and he was right.

Business was conducted through his agent in London, who secured him £3,000 for the photos taken during one hour's work on the beach.

'You know, of course, how you can make megabucks?' the agent offered.

'How?'

'Topless models.'

The Daily Sport paid Ken at least £800 per month, at that time, for this new type of work – the infamous Page Three-type photo. Roughly about the same was earned via his agent, plus his regular weekly salary. Back then, the total was a substantial amount, which meant some kind of security for the family, or would have done if the money had not been gobbled up.

Health and Money Worries

Debts began to mount. By now, Ken had embarked on running courses at his house for topless models. Every weekend men and women would visit for the photo shoots. Olive, his wife, was not altogether comfortable with the venture, though it was to last for many years. She particularly disliked the bad language that one man used.

Olive's health was not too good. Her GP wanted her to see a consultant who then arranged for her to be hospitalized. One day the ward had a visit from a local minister from the Baptist church. The ward sister informed all the patients that there was an invitation from the pastor to join him in a short service in the chapel. Would anyone like to go?

'My arm shot up,' remembers Olive. 'It didn't seem to be me who was putting it up, if you know what I mean. I had been feeling very down that day.'

As she listened to the words spoken by the pastor and from the Bible, Olive was very challenged. As a young girl she had attended church and became a Christian when she was sixteen years of age. But she had let things slide in her life, so much so that she had allowed other things to take the place of her faith in God. But God had not forgotten her and was giving her another opportunity to rediscover her Saviour and Creator. From that day there was a rekindling of her spirit, giving her a desire to read her Bible, pray and witness.

After she was discharged from hospital, the contrast between Ken's and Olive's lifestyles verged on the ludicrous. While topless photography was going on in her home, Olive had become a regular at Lansdowne Baptist Church in Bournemouth. Everything came to a head when she gave Ken this ultimatum:

'OK. You have two choices. Either you give up this type of photography altogether or, if you still want to continue with it, then you must allow me to speak to the men and women who come into our home. You must allow me to tell them about Jesus – how he loves us, died for the wrong we have done and that he wants to give them real Life that doesn't end when we die. Back off or let me speak freely.'

Ken was earning a lot of money from this job. He couldn't see where else he would get the money. He was scared he would have to pack it in there and then. In the end, they agreed that Ken would continue, but Olive was allowed to speak quite openly to anyone in her home about Jesus. Surprisingly, the models and photographers seemed to accept that this was all right. The man with the foul mouth no longer swore in front of Olive. When his eighteen-year-old son died, the first person he phoned was Olive, asking her for prayer.

'When Olive joined the church, I began to persecute her. I allowed her to attend only once, on a Sunday.

Prayer was very important to her. For thirteen years she prayed for me. She told me that a new minister called Steve Brady had been appointed to the church. Steve wanted to meet and get to know all the members so he was inviting two or three couples to his home each night. "Bring a photo with you."'

Ken was invited, but was very reluctant.

Olive managed to drag him along.

'Did you bring your photo? Could I have a look at it please?' Conversation had flowed, making Ken feel more at ease.

'Here is one of the family.'

As Steve looked at the snapshot he commented that it looked very professional. 'Who took it?' he enquired.

Ken confessed that it was one of his own and then went on to tell Steve exactly what his job was. If the minister was shocked, he didn't show it. He had been brought up in the north of England, in Liverpool. Inner-city life was raw; a place where youngsters could not avoid seeing the evidence of the ravages of what the Bible calls sin.

As they talked about Ken's work, Steve shared a story with him. 'A little lad in Liverpool was sitting in the gutter, sucking a rusty nail. When his dad saw him he shouted, "Take that thing out of your mouth. Give it to me, now." The boy took absolutely no notice of his father and refused to hand the nail over. He carried on sucking his dirty old nail. "Hey, son," called his mother appearing from the house with something in her hand. "You give me your nail and I will give you this ice cream." The lad jumped up quickly to make his exchange.

'I don't think I have to explain that story, do I, Ken? You know what you have to do. God is offering you something far better. How about it?'

Ken thought. 'Thanks, Steve, but no thanks.'

Life Changes

In 1992 it was Ken's turn to suffer illness. Internal
bleeding from the bowel had been diagnosed within
three days after tests, examinations and so on. It was not
a pleasant illness. It took the doctors three years to sort
out that he needed an operation. Ken wasn't well enough
to work full time or to do the courses, so gradually went
out of circulation with his contacts in photography. Ken
believes that in a way God used the opportunity that his
illness brought to make it a little easier for him to give up
the seedier side of his work.

Preparations were made for him to be admitted and
undergo surgery. Lying with his head resting on the
pillow, Ken looked round the ward at the busy staff,
poorly patients and the gaggle of strangers emerging
through the doors . . . it was visiting time.

Ken had told Olive that there were two people he did
not want to see: Pastor Steve and Dr John Faulkner-Lee
with his big Bible . . . and within twenty-four hours they
had both visited.

'John came every day, even though I was very rude to
him. One day he brought me a
small gift of a Bible. Hand-
written in the front was a verse
from Jeremiah. "For I know the
plans I have for you," declares
the Lord, "plans to prosper you
and not to harm you, plans to
give you hope and a future" [Jer. 29:11]. I realized that I
was in a big hole from which I could not get out. After
John left, I opened the Bible and read the verse again.
Alone in my hospital bed I prayed to God, surrendering
my life to Him.'

**I realized that I
was in a big hole
from which I could
not get out.**

Ken's illness meant that he had to retire on medical grounds. As a new Christian, he wanted to learn more about God so enrolled on a couple of courses, like Alpha, where over a meal each week he informally chatted with others about the Bible and its teachings.

However, there had been problems with his blood which meant he wasn't getting better. Naturally he and the church prayed about this, but Ken felt that there was still some block between him and God even though the Page Three days were over.

'Ken, what did you do with all your photos, negatives and things from the old days? Did you get rid of them?'

The question from his church leaders made Ken admit that he hadn't. Perhaps he should. There were an awful lot of them . . . 25,000. Despite earning a large amount of money from his work over twenty or twenty-five years, he had still ended up in debt. It had been a waste of time.

Taking a large pair of scissors, he sat down with his collection covering his life's work and, one by one, cut them up. It took ages.

'I know this may seem strange, but some days later I felt something within me say "You're cured," and then again ten minutes later, "You're cured." My next blood test was normal.'

Olive's prayers for her husband were answered after thirteen long years. Ken decided that he wanted to be baptized by full immersion at the Baptist church. Baptism is an outward expression of what has happened on the inside, so does not itself make a person a Christian, but it was a symbol that Ken wanted to identify with . . . that of the death and resurrection of Christ. As he went down beneath the water he was saying goodbye to the old life and rising up again to testify that he had been given a new life in Christ. Ken publicly told his full story to the assembled congregation, which included his sister-in-law. She had never known that Ken had been a photographer of topless models.

Ken smiles as he remembers that day, 'Her face was a picture!'

CHAPTER FOUR

The Addict

Mike had a good friend who was always there for him. This friend was fine company and often made him feel good and confident in front of others. Although this friend could be a bit of a headache, nevertheless there were plenty of laughs too. Unfortunately, this friendship proved to be too much, too overpowering. It got to the point where Mike could never be alone. The friend went everywhere Mike went. Slowly, Mike realized that his friend told lies, was a bad influence and was ruining his health and life. His friend's name? Liquor . . . otherwise known as Alcohol.

Raised in Clifton, New Jersey in the USA, Michael was the youngest in a family of five children. 'I was really looking for acceptance from the rest of my brothers and sisters and trying to compete and compare as I didn't think I fitted in. As I got older, at the age of twelve or thirteen, I started going round with the undesirables. Their ambition was to get themselves in trouble and get chased by police. I suppose it seemed a natural progression to start experimenting with drugs and alcohol. At thirteen I took marijuana. My mother and father drank socially at home, so there was alcohol at home. I would sneak a sip sometimes here and there. As I was growing up, I gradually acquired a taste for it. Not only was I being sneaky behind my mom and dad's back but my brothers and sisters also. This made me feel even more that it was the cool thing to do. I was really searching for love in the wrong places. Addiction grabs hold of you and always wants more, so I kept giving more of myself to lying, cheating and stealing.

'I got to a point in my life after high school when I really wanted to straighten up my act, but I kept hanging around with the crowd. For recreation we got high and smoked pot, took cocaine or got drunk. Deep down, I wanted to break away from that life, but I didn't know how. So I thought that going into the military would probably help discipline my life, so at least the drugs would be done with.'

Mike joined the Navy for three years and, in his own words, 'did pretty good'.

Part of his naval involvement was as a photographer. That was the upside. The downside was that sailors have a notorious reputation for the drink . . . and other things. So besides learning the disciplines of marching, he was also being taught the art of downing liquor.

'I was a typical drunken sailor. My career in the military was cut short in a humiliating way . . . discharged for drug abuse. I did whatever I wanted, just chasing hedonistic pleasures.'

In America, more than in most countries, there is often no embarrassment about talking about one's faith in Jesus Christ. But religion didn't figure in Mike's life. He did have one or two close encounters with Christians though. Some room-mates, who were born-again believers, went to church and invited him along too. 'But all I did there was nurse a hangover I took with me. Another time, as I went into a bar one night, there was a street evangelist who stopped me to explain how I could become a real Christian. He went through some verses from the Bible from a book called Romans. I listened and . . . actually, I understood what the man was getting at, but turned away from it. As I look back now, although I had no desire for God, nevertheless He was placing strategic people around me in my life who were to help change my attitude to Him. (Even an alcoholic uncle of mine was going to be instrumental in my discovering an addiction recovery programme.)'

When Mike was discharged from the Navy his life started spiralling out of control.

'I was now smoking cocaine, although no longer snorting it. My life became just like a fishing line that got all tangled up. I didn't know how to untangle it. I sank into a depression, where the only way out I could see was suicide. I was twenty-five years old. On my niece's sixteenth birthday, when I was sitting alone in my parents' house, I sank to such a depth that I thought about going up to the attic and jumping out of the window. I didn't . . . but only because I feared that I would fail at that, just as I had failed at so many things before.

'I remember once sitting in a bar thinking, "I have been here for a quarter of a century, but what do I have to show for it? Every cent of money I had I spent on drugs, alcohol or women."'

Yet there was a thought that dominated everything else that was swirling around in his head at that time – that there must be a better way to live. 'That was the only thing that I could cling to that gave me any hope. There came a time when I told my parents that I had a drug problem. What emotions they must have felt when they received that news! It was then that advice from an unknown uncle, who himself was once an alcoholic, changed the course of my life. My mother gave me an application form for something called the "Colony of Mercy", which my uncle had given her a few months before he died. I didn't know anything about the colony. I just filled out the application because I knew I needed help. I knew that I had to change my life and, most importantly, I was *willing* to do so for the first time in my life.'

> **There must be a better way to live.**

Mike hadn't known his uncle until he came out of the Navy. Before he died, this uncle wrote him a letter, which included this piece of advice, 'You can go to Alcoholics Anonymous which will get you sober, but it won't get you saved. But it will clear your head long enough for you to decide where you want to spend eternity.' That cut Mike to the quick as he was always searching for something that life had to offer, but always came up empty. When Mike read this letter he thought, 'Where am *I* going to spend eternity?'

Rehab

It was on 7 May 1990 that Mike made his way to his new rehab hostel at American Keswick in Whiting, New Jersey. Nearby is an Air Force base and along the coast beside the ocean is the famous Barneygate lighthouse. A sweeping drive, bordered with neatly kept hedges and brightly coloured plants leads welcomingly to a cluster of buildings blending the traditional clapboard family-style homes with 21st-century brick sports facilities, auditorium and hotel. Adorned with two lakes, Keswick's grounds resemble a small nature reserve. The winding paths among the tall fragrant pine trees, flowering bushes and evergreens enable walkers to spot huge colourful butterflies, insects, birds and . . . snakes!

As well as providing vacation and conference facilities, American Keswick (a charitable Christian foundation) also runs a programme for those people whose lives have been scarred by addiction, whether it be drugs, alcohol, tobacco, pornography or, more recently, food, and sometimes a combination of them all. At the far end of one lake stands the colony building, which is home to forty men who are mentored by 'chaplains' and the staff of American Keswick, whose motto is 'Where God speaks to hearts and transforms lives.'

Mike's reaction on his first night, when all the guys got together to sing hymns, was what had he got himself into? Had he joined a cult? But, as he sat through something called 'devotions', he found himself actually listening to the speaker.

'The world out there will tell you that you suffer from a disease and that there is *no* way of changing your life, that you are stuck with it. In gambling terms they tell you that life has dealt you "a hand" and that is the "only hand" you have to play with. But the Bible says that "If anyone is in Christ he is a new creation" [2 Cor. 5:17]. No longer does he have to be condemned to that old lifestyle of addiction and sin, because "the old has gone, the new has come!" [2 Cor. 5:17].'

Mike remembers how, on that first night as he sat on his bed in his strange room, he went over in his mind what he had just heard. 'I thought to myself, this is for real! . . . and God, if this is real and you can save me,

I give my life to you right now . . . take me and do whatever you want with me.'

That was some turnaround, as not so long before he had been contemplating what a waste his summer was going to be in rehab. This was probably his first ever real prayer, but he meant every word of it.

'I believe that from the moment I cried out to God He began to show me new ways of living. That summer was not a waste after all . . . it was the summer that turned my life around.'

The surroundings may be pleasant, even idyllic, but the daily regime for the colony men is hard and strict. Above all though, it is administered with compassionate love, mercy and understanding by fellow men who have had their own lives transformed by Jesus Christ. No charge is made for the Colony of Mercy programme other than the non-refundable deposit. Each man is provided with a comfortable room, good food, and laundry and linen service. A work therapy component involving six or seven hours each working day is a vital part of the recovery process. No medical or modern psychiatric method is incorporated into the regime. Biblical in orientation, the goal of the 120-day stay is spiritual transformation, which results in freedom from the bondage of addiction. Included in the requirements to which they all have to adhere is commitment to abstinence from all tobacco products, as well as drugs and alcohol. Only life-sustaining medications prescribed by a physician are permitted and are administered only under staff supervision.

Mike found that God had heard and was answering his heartfelt cry. As he read the Bible by himself and discussed it with the staff and other men, he came to understand and believe in Jesus Christ. He discovered that Jesus Christ had come into the world to seek and to save those who are lost: that all have fallen short of God's standard – perfection – but that by His death on a cross, Jesus died as the substitute taking the punishment for all the wrong we have done. And because He rose from the dead He can free us not only from the penalty of sin but also its power and influence in the lives of those who cast themselves on the mercy of God. In repentance, Mike asked Jesus to be His Saviour and Lord, the new boss of his life.

No one wakes up one morning and says to himself, 'Wow, I think I'll be a crack addict today.' Or, 'I think I will be an alcoholic.' But the reality of addiction is that it does take a soul as its prisoner and unless there is help from outside there will always be a lifestyle that is characterized by life-dominating sin. But when a person becomes a Christian, God, by His Holy Spirit, gives us a way of escape and freedom from the bondage of temptation.

'No Man's Land' is the term used by soldiers to describe the ground between two opposing trenches. Sometimes when we are tempted we feel as though we are in the No Man's Land of a spiritual battle. Being accountable is something that most of us take for granted. It's a way of life. We are accountable first to our parents, then our teachers, the police, our boss at work . . . but when life gets messed up, as many an addict will tell you, often there has been little history of taking responsibility for one's own actions. By acknowledging God and his own wrongdoing, Mike made the first steps of recovery from the No Man's Land of temptation. He also made the discovery that God created us with a need for fellowship with Himself first and foremost, but also to be interdependent with friends, personal family and the wider church family.

In the colony, the guys are challenged in their programme, not only by the staff, but sometimes also by their peers, to examine their attitudes and behaviour, although always in the light of what God says to us in His word the Bible. 'Be careful, your reactions are showing!'

Often the men have never known what to do when, for example, anger overtakes them, letting it spill into violence. But, patiently, staff members taught and showed them a better way. Personal discipline, hard work, clean beds and good regular meals all help with the process of rehabilitation.

Mike made it to the end of the programme. He had struggled with the outward temptations of alcohol and drugs. He had become aware of the less obvious snares such as pride, wanting to be the centre of attention, reacting badly when faults were exposed. But he was also not leaving alone – he had a friend in Jesus and consequently in His people in a church who would, and still do, care for him.

He has been free from drugs. He has stayed away from alcohol, though he did test himself with a social drink with dinner, but that led to further drinks afterwards and then down to the bar. Way deep down inside of him, Mike heard that 'wake up call' that said, 'Hey, you don't want to be going down this road again.' It was enough of a reality check to make him realize that he was finished with drink for good.

Postscript

Philadelphia boasts many fine colleges and students. Out of all the graduates one particular person could justifiably be proud of himself . . . Mike. When he started college he was no longer an addict, but he was virtually penniless. Working on campus helped to supplement his student loan and government grant. After his graduation Mike was invited to return to Keswick as a staff member. At the present time, he serves as Director of Addiction Recovery Ministries and the Vice-President of the Christian Addiction Rehabilitation Association. He is married to Carole and they have a daughter, Sarah.

If you have a problem with an addiction and would like help, please contact

In USA:
America's Keswick
601 Route 530
Whiting, New Jersey 08759
Web: www.americaskeswick.org
Email: colony@americaskeswick.org

In UK:
Info@teenchallenge.org.uk

CHAPTER FIVE

The Hairdresser

Liz wriggled her toes firmly in the sand as the icy cold waves splashed up her legs and on to her thin little dress. A sharp intake of breath was followed by excited giggles. This was not part of a family holiday, but the normal routine of a very privileged childhood. Her parents owned a bed and breakfast at Newbiggin-by-the-Sea in Northumberland. The beach was literally at the end of the garden. High tides often provided great amusement for her dad and brother as they could stand in the flowerbeds and fish!

Entertaining was very much a part of their household as, at that time, dad was also the local bank manager. Respectability did not include religion, however. Sundays were spent on the beach, on day trips or visiting relatives. Liz's first encounter with the established church was not exactly the best advertisement. On hearing some peals of church bells one Sunday, she pleaded with her mum to go to church.

'I think she made some excuse, but I continued pestering until she eventually gave in. The church gave each child a pretty little stamp to stick in a special book each time they attended. I quite enjoyed the singing, but had to miss a few weeks due to a bad bout of bronchitis. When I returned it happened to be Easter and all the children were given an Easter egg apart from me because I hadn't been going regularly. I promptly ran back home with tears streaming down my face. When I blurted out what happened my mum's response was, "Well, if that's Christianity, I don't want to know."'

Moving On

Liz and her family had enjoyed and made the most of those early years by the sea. Fond memories of happy times would stay with them for as long as they lived. Sadly, like many in the rapidly changing society in England, it was becoming very common for families to have to uproot and move for employment reasons. The family moved to Leeds, which was a far cry from the salty spray and bracing winds of the North East coast.

Liz tolerated secondary school, but frankly she confesses, 'I wasted most of my time there . . . fooling around and regularly being sent out of the classroom for talking.'

Her natural talents were developing, not in the world of commerce, much to the disappointment of her dad, but in the creative glamorous lifestyle of hairdressing and styling. Saturdays and holidays were spent getting valuable experience with the scissors and the dryer. Liz gained an apprenticeship and attended the local college, which she thoroughly enjoyed and which launched her in her own right as a hairdresser into the salons of Leeds.

Not long after she decided to go freelance and start her own business. Things were looking up. Financially she was also in a position, at the age of twenty-one, to buy property.

Liz loved life. Her new house was always open to friends and neighbours. Her bubbly, outgoing personality expressed itself in the whirl of parties and nightclubs so readily available in cities. Inevitably in that atmosphere, as so many young women find, Liz slid into the excessive drinking which accompanied this great social life. A number of failed relationships with boyfriends subsequently left her with feelings of deepest hurt. What had started out to be so exciting was now tainted by disillusionment with life in general. The whole thing of living to please herself was not all that it was made out to be.

> **The whole thing of living to please herself was not all that it was made out to be.**

Questions would creep into her mind uninvited and unanswered. 'What's it all about?' 'Why am I here?' and 'Is there a God?'

Liz's 'spiritual' thoughts had to lie dormant. She didn't actually know any Christians and didn't go to church, so it seemed that there was no solution for the uncertainty that knocked the edge off her socializing. One day, after a knock on her door, she invited two Jehovah's Witnesses into her house, but as soon as they mentioned that they were against blood transfusions she knew they were wrong and their religion was not for her.

Soon after, however, something amazing happened to her parents. First her dad, the respectable bank manager, and then her mum, became Christians. It wasn't that they suddenly started attending a church so then called themselves Christians (a bit like going to a garage doesn't make you a car!). Rather, something or Someone changed them from within. At first, Liz thought it was just a fad. 'Just like it was with his fishing . . . and golf . . . and other hobbies,' Liz noted. 'But this really affected their whole attitude to life like nothing else before . . . particularly their attitude to people. It was intriguing and I have to say that I was impressed.'

Health Scare

During this time something rather worrying was happening to Liz's health. She was still as active as ever in her day-to-day life, but she had discovered a lump. Looking carefully into the bathroom mirror she moved her hand gingerly over her throat and neck area. Yes, the lump was still there.

Naturally, one's mind runs wild with all sorts of scenarios when confronted with such an unexpected situation, especially in a young woman. What sort of growth was it? How was it going to affect her? Would she have to have surgery? Was it close to her windpipe, the trachea?

Her parents, too, were worried. As soon as possible, they made sure that Liz saw a doctor. After consultation at the hospital, everyone was relieved as a benign cyst was diagnosed. Although not life-threatening, it was still in an awkward position and would have to be removed. A further trip to the operating theatre was also required six weeks later to drain the cyst.

When people at the church Liz's parents attended heard of her operations they promised to pray for her. This really touched Liz. 'I remember thinking "That's nice . . . and they don't even know me."' Among the congregation, by strange coincidence, was a surgeon who assisted at her operation. When he recognized her parents in church he and his wife invited them and Liz to his home for Sunday tea. 'Don't go diving into your food,' Liz's mum warned, 'they are Christians so I expect that they will want to say grace first.' It was way back in infant school probably that Liz had last said grace. Still, it was lovely food . . . and they were an extremely kind couple who had a real love for people and for Jesus. 'I'd never met anyone like them before,' remembers Liz. 'I will never forget our first meeting.'

Her dad bought her a Bible. Liz would pick it up occasionally searching for 'the truth'. She even began going to church. Whilst listening to some of the sermons she actually thought that someone had told the preacher what she'd been up to in her life. But of course they hadn't. 'I know now that it was all part of how God was working in my life, but I wasn't there yet. I came to the point when I knew I couldn't live two lives, so I stopped going to church. I tried to ignore God. The partying with its late nights and drinking continued, but I would come home in the early hours and look for my Bible, asking God to help me find what it was I was looking for. Deep down I was not happy. God was so patient with me, I realize now, for it wasn't until some months later that I decided 'out of the blue' to meet my parents outside their church to go to their house for lunch. Who should see me but the wife of 'my' surgeon. She headed in my direction as soon as she saw me. There was no chance of avoiding her. She asked if I would like to go back to her house that evening with others my own age, to watch an extract from the film *Jesus of Nazareth*. That night I was so moved by the suffering of Jesus on the cross that I began reading my Bible again.'

Not long after, the surgeon's wife invited her to a special event that was being arranged at a football stadium in Sheffield. Liz didn't care much for football, but she found out that the ground was only being used as a venue for some famous evangelist who was going to preach there. Famous personalities, music and interesting topics were also part of the programme. Publicity about it had gone out all over the north, which also generated media interest as well. It seemed as if it would be an interesting night out even if it was a little out of the ordinary. Besides, she was becoming increasingly fearful of one day having to stand before God and give an account of her life.

The consequences of that night were to be profound and far-reaching for at least one person. So many thoughts were racing through Liz's mind as she listened to Dr Billy Graham clearly explain the gospel message to the many thousands gathered in the stadium.

'I can't remember much of what was said, but I knew I had to put my life into God's hands. I was very ashamed of the way I had been living, even though it was quite acceptable by society's standard. The Bible's word for it is sin. But when I compared my life to that of Jesus, I felt so guilty and ashamed of the things I had done. That night, I prayed and asked God to forgive me for all the wrong things I had done. Despite feeling that it was a daunting prospect, I decided to live God's way rather than my own.' Immediately after that prayer, Liz knew that her life would not be the same again.

'I gained an inner peace knowing that God had forgiven me. I battled to forgive myself, but read in the Bible, "their sins and lawless acts I will remember no more" [Heb. 10:17]. I have to admit how wonderful it was to know that God loved me so much that he sent His Son to die in my place, taking the punishment that should have been mine.'

Liz was twenty-four years old.

Lifelong Faith

Those of a sceptical mind might try to dismiss Liz's new direction in life as a fad, just as she herself did when her father became a Christian. Others could have seen it as an escape from life's problems. Liz answers the doubters by confirming that her faith and trust in God today is as strong, if not stronger, as that day in Sheffield when she became a Christian. However, nowhere in the Bible does it say that a true believer in Christ will necessarily experience a trouble-free life, but it does point us to the One who can help us to cope and get through whatever our problems may be.

'For a number of years I struggled with the fact of being single. But I prayed that if God did have that special person for me, He would keep me trusting in Him to provide a Christian husband for me . . . He did!'

Steve and Liz were married in 1993 and settled in a suburb of Leeds. Steve was able to get employment locally while Liz continued with her mobile hairdressing business. Naturally, they and their parents were quite excited when Liz found out that she was expecting their first child. Following the birth of Hannah, however, and after undergoing various investigations, the doctors told Liz that she had 'unexplained infertility'.

'This was a great disappointment to us. I have shed many tears and experienced much heartache, which only women who have lived through this pain will understand and know what emotional turmoil this brings.

'When I reached forty years of age I finally came to accept that we wouldn't have any more children. So five years later, after being infertile for nine years, to my absolute shock, disbelief and delight, I found out I was pregnant. Sadly, within a few weeks I miscarried. I was utterly devastated. I have asked myself on occasions why God allowed me to go through this trial and I honestly don't know.

'Despite this, I know that my days are in His hands; God knows the future and I am glad that I have put my trust in Him. He will see me through the sorrows and joys of life. I am so grateful that even when I don't understand why certain things are allowed to happen in my life, I can still trust in the knowledge that He is my heavenly Father and he knows what is best for me.'

CHAPTER SIX

The Punk
and the Budgies

Joe Donnelly has an enlarged heart . . . but he does not need to see a doctor. Rather, Joe is big-hearted in the best way possible – he loves people. Joe is a fine strapping specimen of an Irishman from Dublin. Meeting him is an experience (as are his jokes). Joe cares a lot. He cares about people mostly. He has a heart for men, women, boys and girls . . . and God. But it wasn't always like that. Oh, and where do the budgies come into it?

Little Joe grew up in true inner-city Dubliner fashion. Despite being in a staunchly Catholic area Joe and his pals found a Protestant mission hall down one of the streets. Despite being warned fatefully 'not to go near the place because Protestants go there and you don't want to associate with them', the boys were curious and naughty. Being a mischievous type of lad, Joe spent his Saturday afternoons pelting the unfortunate building with stones. No doubt the members had a regular contract with the glass-repairer.

Teenage years saw Joe and his mates at cider parties. The stone-throwing had developed into full-blown vandalism. Before he knew it he was twenty-two years of age standing staring into the black murky waters of a canal in Amsterdam . . . contemplating suicide. Where had the years gone? How had life sunk so low?

'A voice was blasting in my ear, "throw yourself in . . . life isn't worth the struggle . . . go ahead it will all be over . . ." Somehow I resisted. I walked away and felt worse walking away from that. Making a decision to end your life and not being able to carry it through is actually worse as you feel such a failure. I came back to Dublin and for the first time in my life I listened to someone who wanted to share some good news with me about Jesus. Before that I never listened . . . I just used bad language, put on an ugly face and frightened people away. I was even proud of how I could frighten people. It was then that I came to the end of myself. Sometimes I think God allows us to get to the point of extremity so that we might be prepared to listen to his voice.

> Making a decision to end your life and not being able to carry it through is actually worse as you feel such a failure.

'One day a fella turned up from Ballyfermot in Dublin from a similar type of background as myself. Having been brought up a devout religious Roman Catholic and as a teenager hoping to be a priest, this fella was now bananas about Jesus. He didn't seem to give a hoot about what people thought about him or what he said. I remember thinking when he was telling me about Jesus

... whatever it is I hope it's not contagious ... imagine ending up like that poor idiot!'

The trouble was that what he had said somehow stuck in Joe's mind. He talked of Jesus being his best friend and in his heart, as well as the love that he felt for God in his heart and how he could express that.

'It sort of irritated me and yet in desperation I wished it could be true. He gave me a copy of the New Testament, which I took home with me thinking "I'll put it at the end of my bed." Because I lived in a devout Catholic family you didn't let anyone know that you had a Bible or read a Bible. That was only for the clergy ... not the laity. So I hid it in my bedroom, as I didn't want to cause any hassles. However, I did try to read it but all the time the voice I had heard in my mind in Amsterdam kept coming back to me ... "don't read it ... you will lose all your friends ... you will go mad."

'There I was sitting in my bedroom; me, Joe Donnelly, a punk rocker, reading the New Testament for the first time in my life. I just picked it up and started to read it. And ever since that time I have read some of it nearly every day of my life. Of course I knew some of the well-known Bible stories such as the Good Samaritan, the Prodigal Son and the bit about the loaves and fishes, but they went into my head along with fictional stuff like *The Wind in the Willows* and Hans Christian Anderson. What was the difference?

'As I was reading the New Testament about this person "Jesus" it was as if an invisible magnetic force began to operate on me. My heart began to warm to this person Jesus. I felt He was amazing. I was prepared to think about becoming a fan of Jesus, not realizing that He calls people to be His followers not His fans. I started to attend Christian meetings at the time. Believe it or not, I went back to the fella who was bananas about Jesus and said to him, "All this can't be true!" My defences were up, but he simply said, "We have been and are praying for you."

'On 8 January 1983, at 9 p.m., aged twenty-three, I gave my life to Jesus.

'Being a typical bloke I had to analyse it and look at it from every angle. After making loads of excuses, it was as if the Lord was saying to me, "You have to take a step of faith here. You don't have all the answers and you don't even have all the questions. Just take a step of faith."

'This is how I came to it. If this man Jesus is alive today, if He is the same person who healed the sick and raised the dead and He wants to come into my life as my friend and Saviour, then OK by me. This man turned the world upside down and He wants to turn my life right side up. So what else could/should I do? I was suicidal. I had found no reason to live. But Jesus said, "I have come that they might have life and have it to the full" [Jn. 10:10]. That is the total opposite to being suicidal.'

A New Life and Community Work

Since Joe trusted Jesus Christ as His Lord and Saviour his world was totally turned round. His suicidal thoughts went. His desire to trash buildings and use bad language disappeared, as his aims are now to honour God and love His people. Joe is now married and has five children.

His full-time work since that time has been an involvement with renovating an old mission hall and developing it into a Christian outreach centre in the heart of the community. Oh yes, coincidentally, it is the same one he used to throw stones at!

But what about the budgies?

Joe and his family had no money, just a desire to turn a derelict building into something useful for God and the community. At first Joe's vision was to build workshops on some of the land at the back. The idea was that the 'drug kids' could restore old furniture and, with the money from sales, help fund the project. However, despite support from friends, Joe felt that God wanted him to do something different. Making furniture was like showing off the work of your own hands; instead Joe decided that the Lord was leading him to work with things God had created. So . . . change of plans. No workshops. Instead up went greenhouses, aviaries and animal hutches. The purpose of the mission hall is to do whatever it takes to bless the community and to share the good news of Jesus.

If you visit Dublin, Joe's mission won't be on the tourist trail, but it is certainly worth a visit. The flowers and veggies, birds and guinea pigs are a treat to see. Things have moved on a bit since the early days. Despite a lack of resources and helpers at the beginning, God has answered prayer and regardless of difficulties the work has grown. There is now a pre-school playgroup that is approved by the health board and meets all government regulations. Kids have regular Bible clubs while the youth all help look after the animals and grow plants. Senior citizens and families all join in too. 'We sell everything we produce. All money, every penny (or Euro) goes to a third world Christian project such as work with street children and hospitals. We affectionately call our work the five F's – fur, feather, flowers, fruit and "fegetables". So you take one of our F's and leave us a fiver!

'A typical scenario is a fella I was at school with (and who helped throw stones) comes and says he wants a budgie for Christmas. He knows the one he wants.

"That's the one over there. And how much are you going to charge?" I say I get them for a tenner from the pet shop and then sell it for twenty Euros . . . you can decide what you want to give me but remember, every bit goes to the third world. I say, "I will leave you alone with your conscience . . . if you try really hard I would give it to you for nothing". . . . He came back and gave me fifty Euros!

'I go round door to door offering people a copy of the New Testament for them to read themselves. I tell them, "Look, it has cost me €2.50 so don't waste my money, please read it." Of course there is always social chit-chat as well. They tell me that the guinea pig needs its nails cutting. I say, "Are you talking about the furry fella in the cage or the fella sitting on the sofa?" So then I show them how to manicure their pet . . . I am their friend. Another house I go to might have a hanging basket like the Sahara Desert. "Nothing will grow in it," they say. "Is there any chance you could put flowers in it?"

'We do it to show people that God is at work in their community. At the age of twenty-two I was suicidal. I think one of the great pillars of the suicidal mind is that nothing is significant. Everything has become *insignificant*.

'To help them understand, I love people to come to our hall. I show them a bowl full of pansies all the same colour, all the same type but every face different. Or I put a two-week-old budgie in their hand. It is just opening its eyes. It is covered in soft downy feathers. To God, that little bird is significant, as is every pansy. I might then go on to say that the Bible says that the earth is full of God's glory. The glory we see replicated in nature, God wants to do better than that in our hearts. The seed is the Word of God. I would then offer them a New Testament to start the whole process. It is so natural and visual. I want the community to see that we Christians are not afraid to roll up our sleeves and get stuck in. Mothers come telling me about sons dropping out of school . . . I say, "Send them down and I will get them cleaning out the rabbits to start with." Animals are a wonderful means of settling them, giving them some responsibility, especially if there is a wayward budgie who is causing all sorts of trouble. The lads love to find a prodigal animal that replicates what is happening in their lives. They not only care for them, but also they begin to open up to me and talk about things they don't feel able to with their fathers. Also the emphasis on caring for others in the third world takes the spotlight off themselves and onto practical, proactive activity.'

Ultimately, though, only God can change a person's heart. But with people like Joe showing real practical love, giving a challenge to the mind and integrity with the good news of Jesus and the word of God, the Bible, our desperately needy society can be changed for the better.

CHAPTER SEVEN

The Policeman

A red saloon car that had seen better days and better owners turned into the forecourt of an east London garage. A mechanic lay prostrate, almost deathlike, beneath an elevated Jag. The only sign of life was the occasional appearance of a grubby hand reaching for a needed tool.

'Eddie! Eddie, have you got a minute?'

The legs under the Jag wriggled until the whole body emerged to face the new customer. This mechanic could take up limbo dancing in his spare time.

'What's your problem, mate?'

'Brakes. Could you have a look at them? I need the car back as soon as possible. Any chance of doing them before the weekend?'

'Yeah. It's quiet at the moment. Better see the boss though.'

'Cheers.'

Eddie wiped his oily hands on a dirty old rag that he picked up from the garage floor. 'How are the wife and kids?' he shouted after his friend.

'Expensive, mate . . . you should be so lucky. Wait 'til it's your turn.' The retort was met with a huge grin from Eddie.

Margaret had always liked Eddie. Having met at the age of fourteen they both ended up working in London. Eddie managed to get an apprenticeship as a fitter for cars and various vehicles. Margaret, meanwhile, secured employment with Norwich Union Insurance, who eventually relocated her far from home in Australia. Not to be outdone, Eddie, too, travelled. His work enabled him to taste foreign life in Germany, Australia and New Zealand. But, as many others find, the pull to come home finally won. He married Margaret twelve years after their first meeting. It must have been love at first sight!

Change of Direction

The risk factors associated with Eddie's job were probably pretty average and certainly would not cause the adrenalin to flow too often. His career change altered all that when Eddie decided to join the police force . . . in Northern Ireland.

Why would anyone want to exchange a 'safe' job for one that was fraught with danger, tension and in a very high-profile situation? The possibility that one could lose one's life was very real. But Eddie loved people. Cars were OK, but he wanted to make a difference in a country that was being devastated by the trouble on its streets. Things were pretty bad at the time. Little wonder that his wife and parents worried at this change of direction. Job security, of course, was a great draw though.

Life was never dull now. No day could ever be described as routine. When a call came through on the radio the pulse would automatically quicken. What might sound like a straightforward incident could turn into something more sinister. The news that a friend and/or colleague had been killed on duty would devastate your day. The pit of your stomach would churn with emotion, but there was only one way that Eddie knew to cope with the realities of the job and that was to put them at the back of the mind. Just get on with your job. Give it your best.

'It does make you think about God,' Eddie reflects, 'but He, too, would be pushed away with the other thoughts I couldn't cope with. The man in charge of my unit was a Christian. I used to chat with him about things sometimes. The police force is a hard place with a macho image. To be a Christian is not thought to be macho.'

Eddie confesses that he was not particularly worried about his personal safety. Some may think him foolhardy, but in all of us there lurks the suspicion that awful things are not going to happen to us. It won't be us in the plane crash or mugged in the street for a small amount of money. Perhaps having this way of thinking enables us to tackle jobs with huge responsibilities that we would otherwise shrink from.

Anti-terrorism and the intelligence end associated with it is not a place for 'softies'. 'When faced with trouble,' Eddie admits, 'I would pray, but it didn't mean much.'

Margaret and he had started one particular day pretty much as usual. Breakfast, chit-chat, plans, a kiss with last words of goodbye, on with the flak jacket . . . and then it was out on normal patrol with six colleagues.

A call went out for them to attend a fire. The driver changed gear and hit the accelerator. Their minds too would have shifted from surveillance matters to dealing with an emergency situation. What would they find? Who would need evacuating?

Suddenly, their thoughts were diverted as shots rang out. Their particular vehicle would protect them from stones that were thrown but not bullets.

Eddie was the rifleman in the back.

'I was hit in my arm, chest and back. I called out to Harvey, "I'm not dead! I am here and I have a flak jacket on." That day, however, I did not put in the metal protective plates that make it so heavy.

'I could see the man who had shot at us coming out of the shadows. He was changing his magazine. He was reloading.

'My colleagues in the front automatically dropped their heads down before the vehicle was hit thirty times. Two bullet holes were discovered about a couple of centimetres above their heads. About five rounds had hit me.'

When they arrived at the hospital, Eddie managed to walk from the vehicle. Only then did he realize that he was bleeding but was not overly worried. It was a different matter when the doctor informed him that a bullet was lodged about half an inch (just over a centimetre) from his heart!

The blokes from forensic later told him that if Eddie had been wearing his metal plates the bullets would have ricocheted and he would have been killed. His injuries, despite being so serious, necessitated a stay of only three weeks in hospital. His arm, which had been fractured in thirteen places, took a much longer time to heal; three years in fact, and then only to the extent of seventy per cent.

It was while he was a patient, lying in bed with plenty to contemplate, that he started to think about what would have happened if he had been killed.

'I didn't want to go to hell. When my brothers and sisters were young we were sent to Sunday school and such-like. Ours was a God-fearing family. I had an awareness of God, but kept putting it or Him off; you know what it is like when you get into your teens . . . football was far more interesting and besides, I played for the local team. Margaret's family were keen Christians who held meetings in their home.'

Once Eddie had left hospital it was all too easy to slide back into how things had been before. For three years, however, he still felt himself under some type of 'conviction' about the afterlife. When he went out for a drink with the lads he would often come home early from the bars. He returned to work after only eleven months off. While his plaster cast was on his arm his duties were lighter, but the time came when he was ready to get back to normal duties and back on his old patch where he had been shot. After six months he was transferred to a different district out in the country. The dangers were not less. One morning he drove out to open up his station only to find that a bomb had blown off the gate and damaged the building. Two hours prior to their arrival a lorry had been passing. The vibrations from the vehicle had set the bomb off. But Eddie still did not fear going to work even after all that had happened to him.

Searching Questions

Family, of course, for the men facing these incidents, is very important. Margaret's parents were extremely kind and hospitable. They would invite all sorts of people to the meetings in their home. Their own son-in-law was one of them. Eventually, he took up their kind invitation and went along one night. People came from round about, from different backgrounds and were different ages. Granddad Totton was by far the oldest, at one hundred and three years old.

He certainly didn't mince his words when he confronted Eddie with some very searching questions about 'getting saved'. The dear old man lovingly told him about Jesus who died on the cross but rose again, having taken on Himself, once and for all, the punishment for our sin. Granddad Totton knew his Bible well, sharing with Eddie familiar verses from Sunday School days that suddenly all seemed to make sense. That night Eddie surrendered himself, all that he had and was, to the God who made him and asked Him to save him.

There was no way that Eddie was going to keep this good news to himself. First of all he rushed back to tell Margaret and Trevor, a Christian who worked with him. In the morning the whole station knew. 'I told them all what had happened and that there were going to be changes. These men had known me for nineteen years. They were shocked.' To become a Christian suddenly after such a long time with them knowing each other inside out, one might have expected derision instead the of the respect he was treated with.

It may come as a surprise to learn that Eddie's two girls grew up not knowing that their father was almost killed by a terrorist. 'I didn't want the girls to grow up narrow in their views. It was only when a lady came to our home and mentioned it that I felt I had to tell them. They were in their late teens by then.' Margaret, his wife, trusted Christ as her Saviour one week after Eddie.

'I know who shot me. He has not been convicted for the crime. If I ever met him I would be prepared to have a cup of coffee and chat with him. I would ask him why he did what he did. Then I would say, "You've told me what *you did* to me . . . now let me tell you what *Christ has done* for me."'

CHAPTER EIGHT

The Power-Lifter

Arthur was a hard man. Outside the nightclub doors his eyes would scan every punter. Always watching – waiting. 'I would pounce like a tiger, seeking the core of the trouble, picking off the source . . . overwhelming the person with my unleashed violent strength. I never failed.'

Being a bouncer for well-known establishments such as Charlie Chan's in Walthamstow, Mr T's in Erith, Kent and The Country Club in Epping earned him enough money not only to support his wife and family – but also to sustain his cocaine addiction. It was almost as though Arthur had a dual personality. At home he enjoyed his role as husband and father. He genuinely loved Jacqui, his childhood sweetheart. But when he donned his doorman's jacket he took on a different persona. Under the influence of the heady atmosphere of nightclub life and all its trappings . . . wheeling and dealing, drugs and illicit sex . . . Arthur found himself being drawn into the dark web of violence.

When Mr Sethers, his gym master at Fairmead Secondary School, encouraged him as a young boy from the local council estate to excel in sport (and particularly athletics) he could never have dreamed what the consequences would be. Arthur was soon a champion sprinter. By sixteen years of age he had equalled the 100-metres national record. Needing to build up muscle, he started what was to become a lifelong passion . . . weightlifting.

His fast-developing body also had to contend with teenage hormones. It was love at first sight for Arthur as soon as he clapped eyes on Jacqui in The Gunmaker's Pub in Loughton. Weddings don't come cheap, so marriage was put on hold until Arthur became an apprentice carpenter and joiner. 'Life for me was good – I had become a man. It was a great feeling . . . but the time had come for me to branch out on my own in work.' Jacqui and he were inseparable.

Wag Bennett's gym was frequented by all the top bodybuilders from all over the world, including Arnie Schwarzenegger. Arthur went along initially to wind down from the pressures of life. It felt good to look in the mirror and see a well-toned body. But more than that, Arthur knew that he was strong, very strong. It wasn't long before he was spotted by a coach who encouraged him to join a weightlifting club. Inevitably, Arthur became hooked by the sport. While on an instructor's course at Bisham Abbey, which is the British National Sport Centre, he was invited to enter national and international competitions. This had never been one of his goals, but he thought he would give it a crack. Soon the medals were beginning to pile up. British, European and Commonwealth records were broken. On the home front Jacqui and Arthur were now the proud parents of Emma and James. Even the business was flourishing.

'I was having the time of my life, but I know it must have been difficult for Jacqui.'

By 1981 Arthur was a regular member of the British team, representing his country around the world. Being treated as a celebrity made him feel even more powerful. Fellow competitors really feared him because he was determined to be a winner.

'I was a force to be reckoned with – nothing could stop me . . .'

The results of a routine medical check-up were a bit of a surprise though – a growth in the back of the throat. But not even that stopped Arthur successfully defending his British title before he underwent surgery.

'A fleeting thought passed through my mind. Am I a mere mortal – or someone who couldn't be touched by human weakness?'

But work carried on at such a pace that it meant that competitions had to be put on hold for a while.

Bad News

The voice on the other end of the phone said, 'Your old man's dead.'

Arthur and his dad had become very close during the last few years they had together. 'The loss of Dad was felt by all. Death is final . . . never before, in such depth, had I confronted the extinguishing of life. The truth was, I had unconsciously assumed that I was going to live forever. Once, when I lifted sixty-six stone, the power that surged through me caused me to not only feel superhuman, but made me feel that I could never die.'

Arthur began to be overtaken by dark, morbid moods. A hip injury precipitated a course of steroids, which consequently led him down the murky path of drug dependence. Having seen what drugs could do to his body beneficially and legitimately, it wasn't long before Arthur was taking amphetamines for mood swings and snorting coke. Supply was never a problem as some of the lifters also dealt in drugs. But financing such an expensive habit meant a bit of a drain on his business even though it was still highly successful. Hard cash was what was needed, so that was when Arthur turned to also being a bouncer at nightclubs and illegal raves. 'As doormen, it was our job to body-search everyone who came on to the premises. This netted us a good booty of drugs for ourselves. When the rave was over, we would divide the spoil. The pay for a night's work was the best I ever got . . . anywhere.'

Arthur decided to pack in his own business as he had become hacked off with all its pressures. It was in the year that saw many changes for him and his wife. A guy called Danny got him quite a good job which included a company car, plus work for Jacqui in the offices. As a life member of the British Amateur Weightlifting Association (BAWLA), Arthur had another go at the British and World Championships. Coming second was a real blow to his ego. 'My appetite for cocaine increased tenfold . . . people used coke as a form of currency. My reputation meant that lines of coke were constantly on offer, and I never refused.' Arthur, the popular celebrity, was about to veer further off course when he met Donna, a tall, leggy girl with blonde hair.

In 1988 he achieved the twin accolades of winning both the British and European Championships. Jacqui, as always, was there for him . . . even when the news came out that he had tested positive for the banned substance, Neandrol. Stripped of his title, Arthur did not contest it for the simple reason that he knew he was guilty. He just joined a different organization that wasn't so stringent with its testing, and went on to become a World Champion.

Unfaithfulness

Coming home brought Arthur back to reality . . . work, family and Jacqui, whom he loved and cared for so much. In return she was always there for him, supporting her celebrity husband with her love. So why did Arthur begin an affair with a woman sixteen years his junior? In the book *Tough Talk* he explains how lying and deception had become part of his life along with his addiction to drugs.[2] Since beginning the door work he had slipped from his normal behaviour naively into the whole world of nightclubbing, drugs, sex and immoral behaviour. As others before him have found, the allure and attraction of an affair became appealing until finally he fell. For a while he combined his marriage and the affair, the latter in utmost secrecy. But eventually the crunch came when he decided to leave his wife and children to go to South Africa with Donna. Their house was sold to buy a smaller one that Jacqui could manage. At first everything was great for Arthur and Donna . . . the beach, parties, drugs and drink . . . until restlessness overtook him. 'Slowly my life was becoming like a hell in paradise. There was still a part of me that really wanted my wife.'

Perversely Arthur left to return to London and Jacqui. His parting words to Donna were, 'I'll be back.'

Unshaven, thinner and looking drawn he was welcomed into the loving arms of Jacqui, whose affection he did not deserve. Despite all his promises though, by the new year he had left his wife and children again. 'Life is a funny thing. Sometimes you can have everything that your heart desires, and yet you are still not happy.'

Arthur, now a notorious debt-collector, was living in such 'darkness' with a very expensive drug habit that drove him to attempt suicide. 'The depressive, suicidal mood that I had drifted into was permanently part of my sad life. There just didn't seem to be any point to anything.' At an all-time low, Arthur finally recognized the fact that he needed help. It came from a most unexpected source.

Macho Arthur had always classed Christians as wimps. It had never dawned on him to 'do church'. When a friend invited Emma, his daughter, to a local community church, Arthur hadn't objected, but could not have dreamt of the consequences of that 'chance' meeting for his life and that of his whole family. It led eventually to Arthur being introduced to and becoming great friends with a bloke called Vin who was a Christian. Arthur was expecting to meet a bearded, long-haired, pebbly-spectacled, sandal-wearing freak! Actually, Vin was quite a big guy who could clearly handle himself OK. Arthur felt some reassurance in knowing that his own knife was strapped to his leg. But Vin was no fool. Despite their obvious differences in lifestyle they struck up a remarkable rapport. Vin didn't preach or rant at him. Together they discovered not only each other's world, but also through the Bible how someone could come to know God for themselves. Vin helped him put his thoughts into perspective, throwing down the challenge for Arthur to make a choice. Was it between wife or girlfriend, his own children Emma and James or a new family, or ultimately, was it a choice between good or evil? 'I had gone from a good life with family and job and peace of mind to a life full of evil, drugs, and violence.'

Hope

Arthur had reached rock bottom. Unable to love others or himself, one day he found himself standing in Spitalfields Market car park. From the depths of his heart and with the arrogance of desperation he called out to God. 'Help me God! Come and sort my life out.'

Prayer wasn't big in Arthur's circles so he wasn't sure if that was how you did it. But he meant it. Nothing dramatic happened. Only a feeling deep within that at last there was peace with himself . . . and God.

The precious knife that was always strapped to his leg was tossed into a skip. In front of his mum he tipped out all his cache of drugs on to the kitchen table. She had had no idea to what depths her son had sunk.

Vin helped Arthur to understand how and why God should love us enough to send his Son Jesus to die in our place so that we can obtain forgiveness and new life in Him. Also Vin was a good friend and counsellor, helping Jacqui and Arthur begin their marriage all over again. At that time Jacqui was not a Christian. She felt she had been deceived and betrayed too many times by her husband. She was tired and had reached the point of defeat with no more fight left in her. But her mum and friend Michelle were always there for her.

'Then,' as she tells everyone, 'Jesus stepped into my life. The work that Jesus accomplished on the cross was paramount in my reconciliation with Arthur. Jesus, who knew no sin, died because of my sin. The time came when I had to make a choice whether to forgive my husband – and put aside the things that he had done, that had caused so much hurt and pain – or not. There was no way I could forgive him in my own strength. Jesus Christ gave me a forgiving heart – his heart. That's how I was able to do it. But more than this, I had to choose Jesus above all else. If I had chosen not to forgive, Arthur and I would have remained apart forever. Forgiveness meant that we would have a chance to be a whole family again, but even if we didn't get back together, I still wanted to have a heart and mind free of bitterness and resentment.'

Would it last? More than ten years on, Arthur is free from cocaine addiction, has a good home life and job and has even competed in and won four British, three European and two World titles – legitimately. But becoming a follower of Jesus Christ won't necessarily mean that all your troubles vanish, or that financial or health worries cease. Rather, you experience the deep underlying truth that, no matter what your circumstances, the joy of the Lord will be your strength and Jesus will help you through.

'No one can argue against the truth of my life. I believe that I am more of a man now than I ever was before. It takes a real man to be a follower of Jesus Christ in this dark, dark world.'

> I believe that I am more of a man now than I ever was before.

Arthur, along with a group of guys from similar backgrounds, founded a charitable trust called Tough Talk. They travel throughout Europe, the UK and the States performing power-lifting demonstrations as a backdrop, while telling their astonishing stories.

If you would like to know more about becoming a Christian or to book Tough Talk please contact them at the address below or visit their website.

Tough Talk
119 George Lane
South Woodford
London
E18 1AN
Email: tough-talk@ntlworld.com
Web: tough-talk.com

CHAPTER NINE

The Businessman

Peter, a young man from the small former mining town of Houghton-le-Spring in County Durham, set off one day on a mission. It was to win the prestigious Aston Martin franchise for his car dealership, founded by his father, Reg Vardy.

The arrival of this northerner at the Aston Martin stand at Earl's Court Motor Show caused something of a stir. 'They were very surprised to see us,' he recalls with characteristic understatement. 'Things were very tough; we were in the middle of a recession. They were finding it hard to sell their cars in Sloane Street, London and therefore were amazed that someone thought they could sell these expensive cars in the North East of England.'

Undeterred by their scepticism, Peter asked that they be given a chance to show what they could do with the franchise. Short of other options and with a need to sell cars, they reluctantly agreed. The result? For the next four years, Reg Vardy was the top-selling dealership for Aston

Martin in the world. In fact, more Aston Martins were sold out of this old mining town in the North East of England than were sold in the whole of North America.

The lesson Peter learnt early on in life was that it matters less where you are than who you are. This ambitious young man went on to become Sir Peter Vardy, successful businessman and sponsor in his local community.

Brought up within a loving stable family environment, Peter could not have wished for a better start in life. His father was a keen Christian man who believed that faith was not just for Sundays and emergencies. It was personal and very real. However, it was the one thing he could not pass on to his children as he would their inheritance. What he did do was tell them about the God who loved them so much. Peter looks back to his mid-teens as the time when he came to a personal faith in Jesus Christ which has guided and sustained him and provided foundational principles for his life and work.

Having passion for people and integrity does not preclude being ambitious and tenacious in pursuit of business goals as is shown in Peter's life. Two revolutionary forces converge in his life with incredible effect. One is that at the heart of every businessman lies someone who refused to accept the conventional norms imposed on their industry, someone willing to break the mould. The other is that at the heart of every Christian is a belief that we have all been created in the image of God, have infinite potential and a refusal to accept the conventional limitations on our lives imposed by society.

Business Success

As Chief Executive of Reg Vardy, Sir Peter Vardy took a small family motor dealership from a single outlet in

Houghton-le-Spring in 1982 to become the most profitable motor retail group in Europe. With a turnover of two billion pounds eventually he employed six thousand people before finally selling the firm in 2006. Rather than disappearing into early retirement though, he now devotes some of his time to help the next generation of the Vardy family, his two sons Richard and Peter, get started in their respective businesses. Peter says, 'One of the challenges of many people with demanding jobs is that they are not able to give as much time to their family as they would like. So it is wonderful for me to have this opportunity to work with the boys and hopefully by passing on my experience, help them avoid some of the mistakes I made in the early days of the business.'

Peter explains that what is required for business success is passionate leadership, total commitment and a willingness to take risks. Far from being a number-crunching autocrat, he has a passion for people and it is infectious. Peter says, 'I always thought great leadership was understanding the strengths and weaknesses of each member of the team, and trying to find a position for them in which they could flourish. People want to succeed and just want their contribution to be valued and respected.' At 'Reg Vardy' he took his pastoral responsibility as an employer seriously. Stories abound amongst staff of his thoughtfulness, generosity and encouragement, which set the tone for the working environment, and ultimately the customers felt it too.

The motor business is, more than most, a people business. Often customers may think that they make a decision based on the features of the car, or the deal on offer, but research has shown that it is the knowledge, attention and trustworthiness of the salesperson that is the decisive factor. Peter knew this and was ahead of his time in developing innovative customer care systems. 'In the early years I prided myself on knowing the registration number of every car I sold – of course when we were selling 200,000 cars a year this was a little more difficult!' But it was this attention to detail and sensitivity to people that he made the signature of his own life and tried to pass on to others.

So why did his business succeed where others failed? Peter would feel that dealerships fail because the leaders do not see the potential of what they have. When the leaders lose the vision, so do the staff. Peter says, 'They start blaming everything from the cars to the manufacturer, to the advertising and it is everyone's fault except theirs. When staff lose their passion for what they are doing, the customers go somewhere else.'

Reg Vardy simply could see potential when others were ready to walk away in despair. They didn't see a poor dealership, they saw a poor leader. Peter quotes his father who would tell him: 'A business will never be better than its boss; it will never rise above its head.' Therefore, the starting point for the business transformation was to show them 'what good looks like'. The managers would be taken to dealerships within the Reg Vardy network, which were in less promising locations, but selling four and five times as many cars as at the failing dealership. 'Once the manager of the business had seen what was possible he had a renewed vision for what *was* possible, and this was infectious on his team,' reveals Peter. The message was plain . . . if the manager had no vision then the business would fail, but with a clear vision there emerged a strategy for realizing it. All of a sudden people are thinking about success rather than failure and it is infectious, eventually touching the customers too.

A Passion for Education

You might be forgiven for thinking that Peter had gone through the usual formal higher education route to get where he is. But his life is an example that, even if you leave school with only one GCSE in music, it doesn't mean that you can't make a decent future for yourself and your family and also leave a positive mark on society. A lesson learned early in his business life was that the only limitations we face are those we impose on ourselves or allow others to impose on us.

Although his business was growing in success, being a prayerful man about everything in his life he sought what God would have him do next. He hadn't anticipated the answer 'education'. 'Surely not,' he told himself. After all, he had left school with a report stating that he was 'unlikely to ever rise above mediocrity'.

He had left school with a report stating that he was 'unlikely to ever rise above mediocrity'.

Then he thought of the lesson of business that the only limitations were those we placed on ourselves, and concluded that if God was in this then he should not constrain divine inspiration with human feelings of inadequacy.

Having always lived in and loved the North and its people, Peter was acutely aware of some of the problems and challenges of the area and of life in general. (He and his family had known personal suffering through the loss of a son in tragic circumstances.)

In 1987 state education was in a sorry condition in Gateshead. The proportion of sixteen-year-olds achieving five GCSE passes or more was under twenty per cent. The proportion of sixteen-year-olds staying on in education after sixteen was only eleven per cent. The Gateshead LEA was one of the worst performing of the 149 Local Education Authorities in the country. Into this 'unpromising' ground the then prime minister, Margaret Thatcher, and Secretary of State for Education, Kenneth Baker, wanted to plant a 'beacon of education excellence' in the shape of a City Technology College. They were seeking a businessperson who would be willing to put two million pounds into the college in order to get it started.

The new college would cater for eleven- to eighteen-year-olds, would be funded directly from government and would be required to take two-thirds of its pupils from deprived and semi-deprived areas. Subsequently, Peter became involved as the principal sponsor of the College while his brother David was appointed project manager.

The plans for the new College met with fierce opposition from those who didn't want to see the local education authority's grip on education provision broken.

Peter admits that the early days were tough.

'We were told that the kids were "thick" and the parents "weren't interested". It seemed as if every possible obstacle was used to block the path to opening the school. We really felt that we were in a battle and were it not for a clear sense of calling that God was going to bless the town of Gateshead through this school, then I would have given up. Against all odds the College was opened for the first cohort of 150 students in September 1990 and was named Emmanuel College, which means "God with us." From the moment we opened our doors we said that we wanted our attitude to be that each child who entered the College was created in the image of God and was worthy of the very best education and encouragement to realize their full potential.'

That was a huge responsibility, but also a fantastic opportunity for the governors, teachers, parents and, of course, the children themselves. The opportunity was grasped and from the outset the performance of the students exceeded all expectations. In 2006 the proportion of students at Emmanuel College achieving five passes at GCSE was ninety-nine per cent, passes at A-level were one hundred per cent, staying on rates for post-sixteen education was ninety per cent and five pupils won places at Oxford or Cambridge.

The performance of Emmanuel College sent shock waves around the educational establishment of Gateshead. Parents would ask schools why their children were not achieving results like Emmanuel. Previously they had been told it was because they were socio-economically deprived, but that lie had been exposed by the performance of Emmanuel students. Slowly the other schools in Gateshead stopped trying to find excuses, and started to learn from Emmanuel's example. As a result the local education authority of Gateshead moved from the foot of the national league tables for academic attainment towards the top. Gateshead is now eighth nationally, ahead of Oxfordshire, Cambridgeshire, Kensington and Chelsea, and up alongside Buckinghamshire.

His former schoolmaster may have been just a little surprised that this 'mediocre' young student would one day hear the words 'Arise Sir Peter Vardy' uttered by Her Majesty the Queen in Buckingham Palace, having been honoured for 'services to business and education in North East England'.

Family Life

Whilst a passionate commitment to hard work is commendable, there is also the need to maintain boundaries in a busy life, especially at home.

'There is nothing like your wife and family for picking you up when you have had a rough day, or keeping your feet on the ground when you have had a very good one.' This response reveals the huge influence his wife, Lady Margaret, and their children, Richard, Peter and Victoria, continue to have in giving Peter purpose for the pursuit of success.

Another boundary for the growing business was church. Whatever was happening during the week, when Sunday came, Peter, an accomplished musician (having been a chorister at Durham Cathedral), would be found at the piano leading the worship at Bethany Christian Centre in Houghton-le-Spring. Church, for Peter, is very much a sanctuary from the whirling events of business. It provides an opportunity to reflect on the priorities of life, giving thanks and praise to the One to whom Peter acknowledges he owes everything.

Not only did his business grow, but so did the church. Eventually a second meeting place was needed, so where better than the aptly named 'Stadium of Light', home of Sunderland Football Club. Peter says, 'We thought it was great because of its name and no one in Sunderland needed any directions. Also, when they get there they see more "Light" on a Sunday morning than they do on a Saturday afternoon,' he adds cheekily.

A cynical general public largely considers the business world to be composed of headline-grabbing high-earners and indulgent ladder-climbing executives. Sir Peter Vardy's philosophy therefore comes to some as a breath of fresh air, but there are always others who are eager to pounce on it as a whiff of religious bigotry. To refute such scepticism you have to meet the man . . . why not try the Stadium of Light in Sunderland, on any Sunday?

CHAPTER TEN

The Singer

A huge Arabic flag hung suspended from a white flagpole just outside Karema's bedroom. As the light breeze caught the folds of the material, making a flapping noise, other sounds drifted up from the backyard and the ground floor. Muslim worshippers were praying and singing in Arabic.

Karema and her brother and sister grew up caught between two cultures. Right from her early years at primary school in northern England, Karema knew that her background was different from her friends. 'My mother was English, but my Arabic father came from the Yemen. Dad was the leader of the Muslim worshippers in his area. Indeed, just before the Second World War, he founded the first mosque in one of England's largest ports. This place of worship was situated on the ground floor of a large house, which also doubled as our home. The houses on either side were bombed during the war, leaving the house I was born in standing alone.'

Many of Karema's childhood hours were spent looking out of her bedroom window listening to her father and the Muslim worshippers, mainly Yemeni seamen, singing and reading the Qur'ān. At the back of the mosque there was a large covered-in back yard where her father would say prayers and sacrifice lambs and goats.

'All the activities of the house were geared towards its central purpose, that of being a centre for Muslim worship,' Karema reflects.

Her dad, who she always called Abba, would spend lots of time telling her stories about God's creation, the Old Testament prophets and his own beliefs. This gave her a sense of respect for him and his loyalty to his prayers and creation. 'He made a great impression upon me which, in turn, influenced my attitude to God's law, moral choices and reverence towards the creator.' Muslims believe in the teachings of a book called the Qur'ān, which was revealed to the prophet Mohammed in the year 610 AD. The Muslim creed is 'There is no God but God (Allah) and Mohammed is his prophet.' Muslims believe in the balance of good outweighing evil for eternal life and forgiveness. They believe that Isa (Jesus) never died on a cross and that he will return and make all people Muslim.[3]

Karema's unusual background taught her reverence for a creator God . . . but she wasn't sure that the faith she was brought up in was the Truth. Her life seemed to be full of loose ends that she was struggling to tie together, such as her place as a female, the western culture that surrounded her and her interest in singing and music. 'All this was troubling me.'

Dreams

Life seemed like a precarious balancing act with Karema trying to juggle her conflicting influences into a continual prayer that God would answer her deepest questions: questions about what he was really like and the truth about him. In her teens Karema had two vivid dreams that she could not ignore. She knew little about anything written in the Bible, but has since realized that verses written in Isaiah and Revelation both seem to relate to these dreams.

In her first dream she was climbing up some stairs on her way to meet God. She felt confident that all was OK, but when she reached the top, God was Jesus Christ and he was seated on a throne. 'I was so shocked and troubled that it woke me up, as if I had had a nightmare.' The next day, while walking with a friend down the high street, a guy in a Salvation Army uniform handed Karema a leaflet to read. The words on the paper were 'Jesus Christ is Lord'. Even more shocked, she threw the leaflet away. In her second dream she saw a man riding a white horse down from the sky, which was full of light. 'I was standing in a dark place where there were large stone pillars.' The rider picked her up and rode off into the light with her. 'I later interpreted this to be Jesus picking me up out of the dark religion I was in and taking me to the Truth.' At this time Karema went to see the film *Jesus of Nazareth*. However, she still did not understand the message of Jesus dying for people's sins at all. She couldn't see the point of Jesus' death on the cross.

Then, through various circumstances in her life, God convicted Karema of her own sin and her need for His forgiveness. Just at the 'right' time she was invited to a bonfire night get-together organized by a group called

'Youth for Christ', where she heard the gospel (good news) of Jesus Christ. She was also given some literature to read including a New Testament. A Christian couple also kept in touch with her.

Gradually, the truth dawned on her that all people need God to save them. They cannot work their way to being good enough for Him. 'I realized I had to trust that God would sort out my future. I did not tell my dad straight away that I had become a Christian, but would gradually have conversations with him. One day we had a third party involved in our conversation and he asked me if I believed Jesus was God. I said I did. My dad was very upset. He said if I had been in the Yemen, I would have been put down a hole, covered over and no one would have mentioned my name again.'

Music

Unusually for someone from a Muslim home, Karema had become lead singer in a local band, which was actually named after her: Karema 4. Maybe music was in the blood. After all, she does have memories of her father singing the Qur'ān in the mosque and at national festivals . . . and of her mother enjoying the latest musical film or stage production. East meeting West – an interesting combination.

Another side to her musical life was the fact that she had met and was seeing the drummer, Dave, who had become a Christian through their talks together, reading the Bible and a book called *Mere Christianity* by C.S. Lewis.[4] They had made plans to be married soon after their engagement, as the atmosphere in her home was unbearable. Karema was told not to return to her father's house once she had left. 'I prayed about the situation, that it would change,' she reflects. 'After a few months had passed I did visit my parents. They welcomed me and we continued to see them until they both died within a week of each other in 1985.'

Throughout their thirty-six years of married life, Dave and Karema's home has always been filled with music. Dave took up the guitar and over the years they have sung about their belief in Jesus at many different venues. However, they have also maintained their involvement in the secular music scene, playing jazz, soul, Motown and folk music. 'I thank God that Jesus' blood bought us the freedom to become God's children, for His Truth and the privilege of belonging to his family.'

CHAPTER ELEVEN

The Aid Worker

'Cooke, you'll never achieve anything. You're a waster.' Hardly the most encouraging remark that a headmaster could give a pupil. Yet young Dave Cooke was to go on to found a most remarkable and extensive aid relief scheme known throughout the world as Operation Christmas Child. Thousands of shoeboxes filled with gifts are distributed each Christmas to needy boys and girls whose smiles more than make up for those derogatory words spoken to Dave all those years ago.

Cooke, you'll never achieve anything. You're a waster.

Dave was quite a handful as a child. He'd often be locked in his bedroom for misbehaving, but would open the window, climb down the drainpipe and run away. His unruly behaviour was possibly a rebellion against the rigid regime he was raised in, where there was no real outlet for his energy. Whatever the cause, however, everyone around him found him very difficult to control. 'I can remember quite a happy childhood, apart from the awful restrictions. It wasn't all gloom, there were happy moments.'

Life began inauspiciously, and literally, in the front room of a little terraced house in Chester, England. Older brother Paul, and two younger sisters Jan and Rachel were greatly loved by an incredible neighbour whom they affectionately called Aunty Betty. Having eight children of her own and a television she was a great attraction! Dave's parents belonged to a very tight-knit exclusive religious community, which meant that he found himself barred from participating in many social and sporting events. 'I had an odd schooling experience, but I wasn't bullied by the other kids. Because I was one of the harder or stronger guys in the class I could handle myself well. I was the clown of the class, which was an attention-seeking ploy.'

Dave's mum noted that he had always been a very caring, loving person. Even as a boy, he was good with smaller children and really looked after them. 'But mixed in with this he was always full of fun and mischief. It was never that quiet when Dave was around.' Dave remembers, 'As a kid I didn't rub shoulders with those who came from the nicer part of town. It was always the lower or the poorer person that I gravitated towards, the ones who had been to borstal and come back. I suppose it is the same now. I'd rather spend time with those type of people than with the hoity-toities or the Hooray Henrys.'

While Dave often found himself at the centre of trouble at school, he wasn't one to hold grudges. Even after a fight Dave would invariably have a fit of compassion and feel sorry for the person he had just beaten up! A brush with the law, which began with petty theft, soon brought him up short. He had got in with the wrong crowd. Fortunately the police didn't have enough evidence so he was never taken to court.

After leaving school at fourteen, Dave became an apprentice joiner, and signed up for a college course that would provide some qualifications to take him through life. Certain circumstances in his life so far had shaped some of his thinking about God. The sudden deaths of two men who had been like mentors to him had caused him to check out his own faith and relationship with God. Another friend died tragically in a shooting accident. Life was very precarious. Whilst rejecting the strict religious regime of the family home, Dave did not turn his back on God. In fact, he realized that instead of trying to fit God into his world, it was he, ordinary bloke Dave, who needed to be slotted into God's vast plans. When the whole family started going to a different local church, Chester City Mission, many things changed for the better in their lives.

'It was thoroughly refreshing to go to church and to be part of a people that seemed to know what they were praising God for, instead of just acting, going through a list of rules and regulations.' It was a place where the Bible was taught without extreme emphases or legalistic views, but where they learned more about the Christ who could forgive their sins and who loved them unconditionally. Dave worked alongside the Chester Youth Council, helping to set up a youth club in his local area. This involvement in youth work sparked off an interest in childcare, particularly with under-privileged kids. Eventually, he managed to get a job as a childcare officer. This stood him in good stead for the work he would be involved in with Operation Christmas Child.

Romance blossomed with Gill, a girl with an incredible smile and amazingly gentle attitude. Dave's dubious reputation was in complete contrast to hers, but nonetheless they married. Life for them had its rough patches and surprises. A business venture turned sour resulting in Dave and Gill and their two children losing their house to the bank. Even more tragically, Gill, who was pregnant again, lost the child. 'Gill stood by me and supported me steadily as our world crumbled around us. She could easily have said, "You've blown everything." But she didn't. She backed me the whole way. I remember living in digs one Christmas with a couple of my nippers, thinking, "What on earth am I doing here?" Everything around me seemed to be falling apart. But you know God is there and He's got His eye on you. You've just got to hang on and pray that God will look after you and your family. It's important that you have strong faith to go forward.'

Operation Christmas Child

By 1990 things had turned around again bringing more security and stability to their lives. This was in stark contrast to the breaking story emerging on the television showing disturbing pictures of the horrors of the Ceauşescu regime in Romania. Images and reports spoke of children living in cramped, squalid hospitals with few medical experts and supplies. Babies were reportedly dying of AIDS, often contracted through infected needles in the hospitals. Orphans were condemned to a life without play, love or care. Dave could not get these images out of his head. One night, while having a meal with friends, he suddenly said to his mate John, 'Do you fancy driving a truck full of supplies to Romania with me?' First thing next morning he approached his brother Paul for help and also Dai Hughes, whose employer was local radio station, Marcher Sound. Before long the whole venture had captured the heart of Wrexham. Between the wholehearted support of the radio station and the local newspaper, *The Wrexham Mail*, they found themselves in the heart of a highly effective PR machine. Dave's sister, Jan, had the brilliant idea of asking children to wrap shoeboxes in Christmas paper and fill them with things another child would enjoy. Operation Christmas Child was born.

Within hours the foyer of the radio station was swamped with nappies, shoes, toys, soap, pans, bandages . . . What had started as a snowball was quickly turning into an avalanche! Ton after ton of medical equipment started arriving. The original plan to take two trucks of aid was scrapped. Eventually, seven lorries decorated with tinsel, balloons and messages plus a team of eighteen drivers and a film crew set off for their three-day hazardous journey at the worst time of the year amid snow, ice and freezing temperatures.

Nothing could have prepared the Operation Christmas Child team for the horror that awaited them when they arrived at the first orphanage. A deathly quiet hung over the first room they entered, disturbed only by the clicking noise of the children grinding their own teeth out of boredom. Urine-soaked cots and the single lavatory for more than a hundred children released an unbearable stench throughout the building. Each door that was opened revealed another room full of children starved of love and affection. The tough truck drivers were reduced to tears and many were forced to leave the room, overwhelmed by an atrocity they could never have imagined. 'One young boy stands out in my mind,' recalls Dave. 'He didn't know what to do with the shoebox when we gave it to him. As we took things out he kissed each item. So overwhelmed was he by the gift that his little legs gave way and he just fainted.'

'We would give sweets to the children and they wouldn't know what they were. Having shown them how to remove the paper wrapper and eat the sweet inside, the team were horrified to see them also doing the same with sweet-smelling soap. These kids had no idea what the difference was!' The humorous moment diffused the sad atmosphere, which was now being replaced by the gift of love.

At one orphanage all the shoeboxes had been given out. The convoy was revving up ready to move on to its next destination. Dave glanced in the wing mirror and saw a young girl standing in a corner, just rocking backwards and forwards in the cold. He radioed to see if there was another box. Someone found one and took it across to her. When she opened it, there was a beautiful doll inside. 'It was as if out of all the thousands of boxes we carried, this box was meant especially for this girl.'

The team also had on board medical supplies for a hospital where things were so desperate that the doctors were tossing a coin to decide who received the last course of antibiotics. Many lives were saved through the drugs that were distributed that day. As Dave walked down a corridor he felt in his pocket and took out a packet of McVitie's biscuits. He offered one to a member of the cleaning staff as she passed by. Gratefully she took it, but what happened in the next few moments Dave found to be totally mind-blowing. Carefully, the cleaner broke the biscuit into six pieces and gave them to her staff. 'It was just one McVitie's biscuit. I gave her the whole packet and she broke down in tears.'

As the team left Romania, Dave was already planning the next trip. There was much to think about, many dreams for the future, so much to do. As the convoy neared Wrexham, they turned the radio on to hear their local station, Marcher Sound, playing Chris Rea's

'Driving Home for Christmas' especially for them. It's a tune that will always provoke special memories for that very first team.

Tough guys, thrown together for a special mission, had witnessed such utter human distress that had reduced them to tears and melted their hearts. Arriving home that Christmas Dave found it hard to come to terms with the materialism of his own wealthy country. The contrast with Romania was so stark. The people there had nothing.

Each one of the volunteers found it a struggle to cope with the emotional pressure as they gave and received presents on Christmas Day. Dave admitted, 'After what we had experienced my mind kept going back . . .' It took him a while to adjust, but he says it is something he's better able to cope with now.

A New Venture

Many years later, after trips all over the world with thousands of shoeboxes filled with gifts, and trucks bursting with humanitarian aid, Dave's deep compassion for children is as strong as ever. The work of Operation Christmas Child has gone from strength to strength, bringing love and happiness to millions of children. Now part of the international charity Samaritan's Purse, OCC delivers aid – and the message of hope that is found in Jesus Christ – to victims of poverty, natural disaster and war around the world. Dave Cooke, the man who was told 'you'll never achieve anything', has brought love and life to countless children throughout the world.

After fifteen years of working with OCC, Dave has turned his attention to a new project, Teams4U, which aims to connect people and places. 'I felt I needed a new challenge and a change of direction,' he says on his website, www.teams4u.com, 'but in a job that would still involve me in working to help children, and at the same time giving men the opportunity to be men.' His experience, communication skills, compassion and commitment are all still being used to help rebuild young lives.

> In a hundred years from now it won't matter what kind of car I drove, the size of my bank account or what type of house I lived in, but that I was important in the life of a child.[5]

For further information about the work of Operation Christmas Child and Samaritan's Purse please contact:

Samaritan's Purse International Ltd
Victoria House
Victoria Road
Buckhurst Hill
Essex IG9 5EX
Tel: 020 8559 2044
Fax: 020 8502 9062
or visit the website at www.samaritanspurse.org

CHAPTER TWELVE

The Actor

'Most people are other people. Their thoughts are someone else's opinions, their lives a mimicry, their passions a quotation.'
Oscar Wilde

Some would say that Andy had a privileged birth. Not that he was born into royalty, although he can trace his ancestry back to the royal dynasty of the Hapsburgs; but rather it was more to do with his place of birth . . . Yorkshire. England's largest county certainly has a lot to be proud of, including its magnificent moors and dales, North Sea coastline and of course its gritty down-to-earth people.

Andy started out in life in a small stone terraced house in Keighley, which shares part of the bleak, windswept landscape with its more famous neighbour, Haworth, home of the Brontë sisters. Such an inauspicious beginning was more akin to his other ancestors who were Irish farm labourers.

Later on his family moved to settle in a more affluent part of West Yorkshire, in Ilkley. This pretty little town draws many tourists throughout the year. It hosts many events in keeping with its history and local talent. Andy didn't get involved with the traditional Morris dancers, but from an early age was involved with the well-known amateur dramatics company, the Ilkley Players. His most notable part was that of a fire-eating juggler, performed at the prestigious and spectacular open-air Minack Theatre on the Cornish coast.

This taste for acting continued and developed as he made plans for higher education. Leaving behind the gritty, friendly, 'call a spade a spade' Yorkshire folk and accent, Andy headed further north to the granite and oil city of Aberdeen in Scotland. The ancient and excellent University of Aberdeen quite rightly boasts of its achievements by its 'sons and daughters'. But for Andy, the whole role of the academic was exceptionally unappealing especially as in Scotland the degree courses take four years instead of the usual three in England. Still, it gave him more time for those extra-curricular activities such as frequenting the pub, casino and the football ground. Freshers' week is the shop window for the students to be involved with and/or to continue to develop already acquired skills in sport, the arts and a whole plethora of physically and mentally stimulating activities. Andy naturally gravitated to the society whose interests had already captured his heart and imagination . . . the university drama society. Ultimately, he went on to run this influential group. Opportunities arose with a local TV station which invited him to participate in a programme about student life at the university. Other media openings came along with satellite television companies asking him to make films for them. He acted in, and also directed, a number of productions at the Edinburgh Fringe Festival over a four-year period.

Somewhere along the line Andy did also manage to graduate with a 2:1 honours degree. But it was acting that remained his great passion. Whether or not he took off his 'mask' in life is debatable. Perhaps life was an ever-changing play in which he was acting every part with a mask for every occasion?

Once, towards the end of his time in Aberdeen, he lowered his mask for a while. The hallowed turf at Pittodrie was taken over, not by sports fanatics, but by Christians and others who came to hear the famous preacher Billy Graham. Andy, too, went along although the whole thing was so foreign to him. He came to the conclusion that Christians were lovely people but clueless socially! His flatmates must have wondered what on earth was happening to him to make him go to such an event, as it was just not like him. They knew that he hadn't lost the plot but maybe 'times they were a' changing'.

Gambling

'The latter part of my time in Scotland was spent working on a gambling system with a friend of mine. Casinos always appealed to me on a number of levels. As a student, the "free" food was an attraction; the fact that it often cost £100 in losses didn't seem to matter . . . it was free at point of sale. Casinos were places of dreams, real escapism for me. Chasing fantasies was far more compelling than climbing ladders one rung at a time. So when my friend suggested taking our roulette system to the USA where table antes were much higher, it seemed like a sensible career move. And life continued to happen to me. No plot, no plan. Just a series of distractions. Nothing mattered as long as I continued to maximize and entertain *me*. Looking back I can understand

Groucho Marx when he said, "I don't want to belong to any club that will accept me as a member."'

They flew into Atlantic City with his friend full of expectation, Andy still full of himself, although his interest was waning. 'During our stay in hotels while working our system by day and living it up at night, I began to look a little closer at my life. It was becoming increasingly apparent that my life was hollow. I remember, at the height of our winning run, my friend saying, "You're not happy Andy, are you? Even with all this lifestyle and money, you're not happy, are you?"'

> I just knew I hadn't 'arrived' at my life's destination. I felt the main event was yet to come.

At night the lines from Simon & Garfunkel's song, 'Homeward Bound', kept reverberating in his mind as he tried to get to sleep. 'But I didn't mean home in the terms of the UK; I just knew I hadn't "arrived" at my life's destination. I felt the main event was yet to come.' It is said that there is only one winner in gambling . . . Andy was to discover the sad truth of this. 'My friend and I were penniless, sitting on an Atlantic City boardwalk, totally broke with not even enough money to make it to the airport, when a homeless guy came up to us and said, "Have you got any spare change?"' The irony of it all brought a smile to Andy's face. Eventually they did manage to get back home to England.

A New Role

The stark reality of day-to-day living – and working – was a bit of a shock to the system after the glamorous environment of gambling establishments in the USA.

'Real life had arrived at my door and I didn't like it. So I chose a cop-out route. I applied for a PhD and research fellowship in Environmental Business with the University of Plymouth to delay the inevitable. At first this seemed like a dream job. You could determine your own hours of work, write the odd paper or book, give a paper at a conference and generally amuse yourself. The cynical side of me would wonder, having been in this environment for some time, how many of the academics were actually doing something useful! Most of the time is spent creating new worlds of influence. They start by making up a new word. In my case, two – "bioregional regeneration". Then they establish a new journal to promote the new "model". Having successfully created a new world, the next stage involves setting up a conference (somewhere exotic preferably) and then publishing the papers at the conference in their journal. The really successful academics can then remodel themselves by creating another new "model" or neologism (coined phrase) and it all starts again. This was my new role, a part I played with diminishing conviction for seven years.'

Andy also had a fling with politics by becoming the press secretary for South West Green Party at a general election. Outwardly his lifestyle could have caused envy in some unless they had actually seen the turmoil going on inside. 'By now I was drinking far too much. I was becoming tired of self-promotion and the superficiality of life . . . I was longing for some substance, some meaning . . . anything to satisfy the emptiness in my soul. My reading into world religions and philosophies had drawn blanks. But everywhere I went I seemed to come across a Christian. Coincidence or planned by God? I felt that I was playing a series of different parts in the play of life, from highbrow academic to gambler, to drinker, chess player to country club golfer, politician and film-maker to actor.'

Behind the Mask

The people at Mutley Baptist Church became used to this chap called Andy who had been dropping in over the past few months. He always slipped into the back seats but disappeared 'before anyone could "collar" me and make me like them,' Andy recalls.

One night in November was different, however. It was special for the church because several people were being baptized by full immersion in water. Baptism is an ordinance commanded in the Bible for believers as a sort of badge that as Christians they are dying to the old self and now living for their new life in Christ.

The preacher, Ian Coffey, also asked if anyone else wanted to become a Christian. He had explained that Jesus was the only way to God [Jn. 14:6]; that Jesus had died to pay the penalty for our sins, rose again from the dead as living proof and Jesus invites men and women, young and old to come to him for salvation.

Something happened that night to Andy deep in his soul. He responded to the love of God by committing himself to God. After quietly asking God to forgive his sins, he accepted that he had been rebelling against God's ways but that from then on, with God's help, he would be committed to live differently. 'It was awesome! My heart and mind were absolutely captivated by God. I was so hungry, not for physical food, but for spiritual food.' The ideal chap to help Andy was a guy called Adrian from a different church who had time, patience and knowledge of the Bible.

Friends and family must have wondered what had happened in his life. No doubt they thought it wouldn't last . . . but that was twelve years ago!

'Since becoming a Christian, I have been levelled, broken, healed and restored. The masks were taken off one by one until there was only me left. And what was left was not worth looking at . . . but to God I was special. He has a plan for my life. He has been building my life and my character for His purposes ever since. Getting to know God better is the key to understanding life and why things happen as they do.' Andy is now married to Allison and they have three children. 'Being a father, you can't live a life of pretence. The audience is so close, they spot the fake!'

CHAPTER THIRTEEN

The Astronaut

President John F. Kennedy challenged the United States to commit itself to achieving the goal, before the decade was out, of landing a man on the moon and returning him safely to the earth. No doubt thousands of children (and adults too) looked up longingly at the large silvery object way up above them in the starry sky, wondering about and dreaming of walking on the moon. James Irwin was one such boy – with a difference. His dream came true. He became the eighth man out of only twelve to actually walk on the moon.

James didn't have an instant love affair with flying. Sure, he was in the Air Force, but he would have had a career in the Navy had he not dropped out, as he didn't want to spend months away from his family. He did have fleeting thoughts of living a quiet and comfortable life working with a commercial airline, but instead stuck with the Air Force. Learning to fly was something of an uncomfortable experience, though he was never physically sick. His own personal assessment was that he considered himself 'average with no particular aptitude for flying'. Ed Siers, his instructor, was a great guy in helping him get his wings, despite Jim's rather laid-back attitude compared with the other guys. But it wasn't until Jim finally flew solo that he felt he was in his element. The solitude was a complete joy for him.

'I flew better when I could get up there in the sky, close to God all by myself.'

His career in the Air Force began when he arrived at Yuma, Arizona. When he saw all the P-51s on the runway, 'All the tedium and boredom and everything else I had been trying to escape was behind me. I was hooked.'

James was not the perfect pilot, however. Often grounded for violations and being almost wiped out in a terrible air accident, James feared he might never be allowed to fly the top-secret YF-12A. This was every test pilot's dream. But as he had suffered amnesia and concussion in his accident, the authorities were not about to let James fly expensive machinery. Two broken legs, a broken jaw and head injuries didn't appear to be good preparation for one of the most dangerous journeys facing man. Not only that, his age was also against him. By the time he had had his evaluation and further flying experience James was facing yet another hurdle to get over if he was to become an astronaut – his age. Who would pick a thirty-six-year-old near the end of his career? In 1963, his first application to NASA (North American Space Agency) was turned down. The second attempt was thwarted, as they were only recruiting scientists with doctorates so he didn't qualify. His medical history and age were also stacking the odds against him being chosen.

Into Space

In 1966 James made a final desperate effort to become an astronaut. His boss at Air Defence Command in Colorado Springs spoke up for him. Whatever was said must have been quite powerful as James Irwin was selected to become part of an elite team of America's astronauts. This was the highest human honour James could imagine. But it was not until after his Apollo 15 flight that he appreciated other aspects and dimensions of the unique experience that was to be his.

Before James and his fellow astronauts could make their epic voyage, much vigorous training had to be undertaken. Besides intensive college training, James had to learn how to fly helicopters and a variety of planes, how to scuba dive . . . how rockets work . . . orbital science . . . spacecraft design . . . geology . . . maths . . . science . . . plus all the athletic and physical workouts! No wonder it took five years to prepare.

Weightlessness is a phenomenon of space travel, so how did they train for that? One way is to fly a plane high up above the earth and then push the plane's nose down – like a rollercoaster going down a steep incline – then for thirty seconds you will experience weightlessness. The astronauts repeated this manoeuvre hundreds of times. Sometimes they felt sick, but it was great fun floating around the cabin.

Another memorable experience was being in the centrifuge machine. This contraption spun them round in a circle, very fast, in order to allow them to feel the pressures they would experience during the launch and return to earth. James described the feeling as 'the same as having an elephant sit on you!'

The Apollo 10 mission was to be the final dress rehearsal for a moon landing. James was assigned to support the crew. This included making sure all the equipment worked, and also supervising the building of the rocket and spacecraft. Apollo 10's success meant that two months later, via Apollo 11, Neil Armstrong became the first person to walk on the moon. 'That's one small step for man, one giant step for mankind' were the famous first words uttered from lunar soil. James was slowly edging towards his own historic moment by becoming back-up for Apollo 12. He trained along with the crew, ready to step in should one of them be unable to fly – but he wasn't needed.

Space travel is very dangerous, which is why there is so much training, meticulous checks and tremendous preparation. Apollo 13 should have been the third craft to land on the moon. But when an oxygen tank exploded and severely damaged the service module, plans were changed. No lunar landing. Instead the crew faced a dangerous return journey. Back in Houston the team were doing their homework, rapidly doing experiments and then relaying instructions to their colleagues up above. Amazingly, there were no casualties – this time.

In 1969 James Irwin was selected to fly to the moon as part of the Apollo 15 crew along with Dave Scott and Al Worden. When the door of their spacecraft *Endeavour* clanged shut just like the sound of a dungeon door in a film, they knew it was for real. The waiting was over. They were going to the moon!

Looking out of the window, the blue sky got blacker and blacker as they left the Earth's atmosphere. Within twelve minutes they were in orbit more than one hundred miles above the Earth. At that speed they can go round the Earth in just ninety minutes. It would take them three days to fly to the moon.

After orbiting the moon for a day, Dave and James put on their suits and transferred to the lunar module, *Falcon*.

Dave was the first to go down the ladder. James came next but got stuck in the door! He wriggled free, although when his foot touched the lunar surface, he lost his balance and started to fall. All he could think of at the time was that millions of people around the world were watching him in that most embarrassing moment. Fortunately he managed to fall to the side, out of the camera's view.

Whilst admiring the beautiful lunar mountains lit by sunlight, James was reminded of a favourite verse from Psalms: 'I lift up my eyes to the hills – where does my help come from?'(Ps. 121:1.) 'Of course,' James joked, 'we get quite a bit of help from Houston!' But he was also aware that he was getting help from his Creator – the One who made the very ground on which he was standing. However, whilst on the moon making history, James also had an overwhelming sense of the presence of God. He felt that God was calling him to Himself and was going to give James a new mission when this job was done.

Dave and James were the first astronauts to drive a car on another planet. The vehicle cost eight million dollars to build and test! After completing their assignments (plus a few hitches) they began packing up for the trip home. James Irwin left a plaque on the surface in memory of fourteen NASA astronauts and USSR cosmonauts who had died. Also left was a tiny, man-like object representing the figure of a fallen astronaut or cosmonaut.

Re-entry

The trickiest moment in space must surely be the Trans-Earth Injection Burn. This is when the spacecraft re-enters the earth's atmosphere. The slightest error could send it off into space or cause it to combust. Furthermore, it has to be done while behind the moon, which means that there can be no communication with Houston. Everyone on the ground anxiously watches the instrument panels and listens during an eerie silence waiting for the commander's reassuring words that everything is OK. Apollo 15 did land safely. Having become celebrities, it was not long before the astronauts were meeting the President of the USA and travelling around the world on speaking tours.

As a young boy James had become a Christian but, on his own admission, as he grew up he didn't stay as close to the Lord as he should. Now James had explored outer space where he experienced a close encounter with God the Creator and his Saviour. The inner space within a human heart, the spirit of man, is also important to God. God's perfect plan was manifest when he sent his Son Jesus Christ to die for us, to forgive our sins, and to show us He has a plan for our lives.

> The inner space within a human heart, the spirit of man, is also important to God.

James wrote, 'I think there are things that God does not intend us to understand, things that man is to take on faith. Believing in the Creator and taking Him at His word is a matter of faith. But the Bible teaches that the very heavens declare the glory of God, even His eternal power and Godhead, such that man is without excuse. Man was designed to respond to his Creator. The Bible teaches that Jesus Christ, the second person of the Trinity, was the very Creator of the universe.'

Colonel James Benson Irwin died on August 8, 1991 aged sixty-one.

Oh! I have slipped the surly bonds of Earth
And danced the skies on laughter-silvered wings;
Sunward I've climbed, and joined the tumbling mirth
Of sun-split clouds – and done a hundred things
You have not dreamed of – wheeled and soared and swung
High in the sunlit silence. Hov'ring there,
I've chased the shouting wind along, and flung
My eager craft through footless halls of air . . .
Up, up the long delirious, burning blue
I've topped the wind-swept heights with easy grace
Where never lark nor even eagle flew –
And, while with silent lifting mind I've trod
The high untrespassed sanctity of space,
Put out my hand, and touched the face of God.

Pilot Officer John Gillespie Magee, Jr.
No.412 Squadron, RCAF
Killed 11 December 1941

Inspired by the words of this poem, 'High Flight', James founded a unique foundation of the same name dedicated to giving hope and inspiration to the next generation of adventurers, a legacy to young and old, with the message to never give up on noble and Godly dreams.

Jesus walking on Earth is more important than man walking on the Moon.

To contact High Flight Foundation write to
High Flight Foundation
PO Box 62532
Colorado Springs CO 80962
(719) 282-9885

By permission and with grateful thanks to the family of Colonel James Irwin.

CHAPTER FOURTEEN

The Graduate

'Legal writing is one of those rare creatures, like the rat and the cockroach, that would attract little sympathy even as an endangered species.'

Richard Hyland

James's story, although at times entwined with the legal profession, is not an example of the above. Rather it is an examination of a revelation very close to home. Tracing one's family history has become increasingly popular with the easy access to documents via the Internet, plus popular films and programmes such as *Roots*. It so happened that James was at a family wedding in the summer of 2002 where he was catching up with many obscure relatives. Making conversation with one of them James remarked that he attended church and wondered if the relative did the same. An innocent remark. The reply, however, came as a shock. 'No, we're Jewish. As are you!'

'My parents had separated and divorced when I was still quite little. Both of my parents were (and are) ethnically Jewish, though neither of them practised any form of Judaism. My mother had grown up as one of an "assimilated" Jewish family.'

Though ethnically Jewish, the family had, a couple of generations back, chosen to hide their Jewish identity, and had abandoned all forms of Jewish worship and expression. Many in the family attended Anglican churches, rather than synagogues. As James discovered, this has been a common phenomenon in the Jewish world over the centuries, as Jewish people, seeking escape from anti-Semitism, have hidden their true identity. James's mother had remarried when he was only six, this time marrying a non-Jewish man. At no time did any family member reveal James's Jewish identity to him. It was no wonder then that, if anyone had asked him, he would have called himself a 'Christian'. After all, he grew up in Christian boarding schools, where he was required to attend chapel regularly. To be honest though, James did find it rather dull. That wasn't to say that James was an atheist. 'I certainly believed that there was a God out there . . . somewhere. At the secondary school I attended, most boys would get confirmed between the ages of fourteen and seventeen. Many boys, myself included, chose to get confirmed as a social ritual, rather than out of any genuine conviction. It was supposed to be a ceremony that confirmed someone's Christian profession but sadly, as in my case, it is also administered to those who are not genuine Christians.'

As part of the preparation for getting confirmed, James attended classes with the school chaplain. 'We would look at the records of Jesus' life in the Bible. I had read parts of the Bible previously, and if asked, would probably have said that I believed Jesus was God's Son (though I wouldn't have been able to justify this belief.) At one of the classes I was given an article which argued that, if Jesus had not been God, then He could only have been a madman, or a liar. He could not simply have been a good man or a great teacher, for good men and great teachers do not claim (as Jesus did) to be God. This made sense to me and gave my chapel attendance a little more meaning.'

For James, however, this remained a purely intellectual belief and had little impact on his daily life. During his A-level years, he still managed to enjoy the football and beer along with his peers whilst trying to study hard for his ambition . . . to win a place at Oxford University. 'Though I called myself a Christian, God didn't really get a look in much of the time,' he recalls. Nevertheless, something must have been stirring in his conscience. 'I was becoming increasingly aware of the gap between my profession of belief in Christianity and how I was actually living. I remember thinking that I wanted to sort this thing out when I went to university, and included a Bible in my luggage when packing.'

> **Though I called myself a Christian, God didn't really get a look in much of the time.**

Finding Faith

Various societies advertise their meetings vociferously during the first weeks of term, particularly in the hopes of attracting the new undergrads. 'Early in my first term, I attended one run by the Christian Union (CU). Someone who was there started talking about "knowing God". This intrigued me: though I believed there was a God out there somewhere, I certainly didn't know Him in a personal way as this man claimed to know him.' Being curious, James attended CU meetings during his first term. He enjoyed the meetings, though he admits he didn't understand a huge amount about what was said.

In the second term the CU organized some special events at which the Christian message would be explained. Everyone was encouraged to invite friends along. James was rather reluctant to do so, but did attend himself. 'The speaker mentioned the fact that he had a personal relationship with Jesus Christ. This seemed attractive to me, though as yet I didn't really understand what it meant. After one of the talks, the person sitting next to me (called Chris) greeted me and we started talking. I told him that I thought that to be a Christian meant having a belief in God, trying to be a good person, and hoping that, if I was lucky, God might let me into heaven when I died. Chris, however, explained to me that this was not the case. Despite my occasionally religious exterior, I had lived my life independently, in rebellion towards the God who made me, and I therefore deserved God's judgement. Yet Jesus, who had done nothing wrong, had died on the tree on my behalf, taking God's anger in my place. If I relied upon Jesus' death, Chris explained, I could be assured of God's forgiveness and of a place in heaven when I died. I thought, wow, that is so amazing!'

Over the next few weeks other things began to fall into place; the fact of the resurrection, that Jesus really had risen from the dead. Therefore, it *was* possible to know Him personally. 'I remember sitting down in my room one Saturday afternoon, reading a book called *Basic Christianity* by John Stott.[6] (I had turned down the chance to watch a football match, which on reflection was a bit of a miracle in itself!) As Stott explained who Jesus was, why He had died and rose from the dead, my understanding grew. Finally, Stott wrote about a choice I needed to make. I could accept Jesus as my Lord and follow Him in a real way – not simply paying lip service to Him on a Sunday, but living my whole life in obedience to His commands – which would be difficult and costly. I might be misunderstood or even rejected by others. Alternatively, I could reject Him, which would probably mean a much easier life. Either choice would have consequences. To accept Him would mean assurance of heaven and eternity with God. To reject Him would mean that I remained under God's anger, and would face an eternity in hell, under God's judgement. The decision seemed clear, and so, on 3 February 1996, I prayed to God, asking Him to forgive my rebellion, accepting Jesus as my saviour and Lord.'

James's life began to change. His religious exterior was replaced by a genuine desire to attend church weekly and hear the Bible explained. His previous vague belief in God was replaced by a personal relationship with Him. This did not always mean an easy life, but at its best it has brought him great joy and peace.

James graduated with a degree in history from Oxford in 1999, and moved to London to study at law school. After finishing he moved north to Birmingham to commence work as a trainee solicitor. It was at this time that James discovered his Jewish roots and gained a new identity. But how did this square up with his faith in Jesus? For a start, he was not the only Christian in the family as he soon discovered. Apparently, a cousin, Richard, was teaching at a Christian theological college! This intrigued James. Shortly afterwards they made contact.

Dual Identity

'For the first time, the family background and my own Jewish identity began to become clear to me. Consequently,

I began to appreciate in a new way the references to the Jewish people in the Bible. When the apostle Paul wrote of a "remnant" of Jewish people who believed that Jesus was the Messiah, I realized that this remnant included me! Reading Paul Johnson's *A History of the Jews*, I was struck by the many examples of how the Jewish people had suffered at the hands of the broader church over the centuries.'

In 2003 James would have been content to stay in Birmingham, but because the legal market in the city was flat at that time, he secured a job in Leeds. There he was able to attend not only church but also meetings with other 'Messianic Jews': Jews who had accepted Yeshua (Jesus) as Messiah. Initially, this was more out of curiosity than anything else. At LMF (Leeds Messianic Fellowship) the songs and prayers are in Hebrew and English; the sermon looks at an aspect of doctrine or a book of the Bible from a Jewish perspective and *kiddush* is observed at the end of each meeting.[7] (*Kiddush* is a small meal of bread and wine with which Jewish people mark the start of the Sabbath every Friday evening.)

The organizer, Richard, explained the rationale to him. The aim was to provide a setting where Jewish people could come to hear about Jesus in a comfortable, non-threatening environment, without feeling that they needed to discard their Jewish identity. Given what he was learning about Jewish history, it made sense to him. 'As I continued to attend LMF, the liturgy became more meaningful. It was a joy to celebrate the Jewish festivals of Rosh Hashanah (New Year), Hanukkah, Purim, Tabernacles and Passover. I saw how these festivals pointed towards Jesus, the Messiah. I continued to read up on Jewish history, certain books impacting me deeply. As Richard explained, "Jewish believers in Jesus are the 'ultimate' minority". Some unexpected correspondence with my father, who sent my Hebrew *bris* certificate (presented to the parents after circumcision) to me, reinforced my growing awareness of my own Jewish identity, and that I too was one of this "ultimate minority". From early 2004, I started to refer to myself as a Jewish Christian or Messianic Jew. Some Christians were surprised; most were at least mildly interested. Some asked me about Israel and Judaism – I had to disappoint them with my lack of knowledge! Thankfully no one was openly hostile, though there was some misunderstanding: "So you used to be Jewish?" was the question of one man. Explaining the complicated background to my Jewish identity, I assured my questioner that I could be Jewish *and* believe in Jesus. They were no more incompatible than being English and believing in Jesus!'

In 2005, James had the opportunity to visit the German city in which some of his ancestors lived before migrating to England. His family had at one stage been influential within that area, funding the synagogue and setting up a bank. Yet not all had managed to leave Germany; discovering that some thirteen members of his family had perished in the Holocaust was a sobering experience.

'And so, today, I consider myself 100 per cent Jewish and 100 per cent Christian: a Messianic Jew, following in the footsteps of the apostles and the first Christians. As hostility to both Christians and Jews rises in today's society, this sometimes feels lonely. My family, mindful of the fate of some of our ancestors, has also raised eyebrows at the prospect of me declaring that I am a Jew. I am aware that I need to be careful that I do nothing to endanger them. Yet the Jewish people retain a special place in God's plans (Rom. 11:25-26) and Jesus is the Jewish Messiah: how could I deny either?'

CHAPTER FIFTEEN

The Buddhist

'My family was traditionally very strongly Buddhist as far back as is traceable. I was raised on their principles even though we weren't frequent visitors to the temple. (Only major Buddhist holidays could coax my father to temple!)' It had never occurred to Chandrika to question this faith, until one day . . .

A couple of years ago, out of the blue, curiosity prompted Chandrika to explore other people's beliefs. She read about Hinduism, Jainism and obtained a brief overview of Islam from some friends. With the passage of time, however, her interest in religion subsided until she gave the subject little further thought.

While living in England working part-time for a major utility company, Chandrika became friends with a bloke at work. Rob was a bit different to a lot of guys as it turned out that he was quite open about being a Christian, and was a person who seemed to hold quite strongly to his faith. Naturally, things kept coming into conversations. Sometimes he would pass on to her some Christian leaflets.

'Reading the literature gave me a completely different perspective to Christianity.' Rob was a great one for giving her 'dares' (at this time dares were quite irresistible to her . . . no doubt relieving the tedium of work). One dare was a challenge to read the Bible. 'Normally, at this point I'd have satisfied my curiosity and moved along to the next topic of interest. But this time it was different – something had changed. I had flipped through a Bible briefly when I was about fourteen years of age. But now I felt guilty to even be in possession of a Bible, let alone read it. For two days I didn't open Rob's Bible – until the urge to find out more got too powerful. I started off with the first book of the Old Testament – Genesis. It was not easy going. I didn't understand some of it; I had doubts about other parts. I'd discuss my progress (or lack of it) with Rob on a daily basis, when he would encourage me to read the Gospels in the New Testament. I resisted for a week or so, thinking that starting any book in the middle was a great way to get confused! Finally, I started on Matthew's Gospel. The ease with which I followed it came as a surprise to me, as did the fact that I was even understanding it. It was actually making sense.'

Rob was bombarded with more questions, more discussions. He was very patient. Chandrika comments, 'I was still receptive to more information . . . my personal beliefs were still steady and Christianity was still non-threatening. At the back of my mind were my parents. Open-minded though they were about most things, an in-depth look at Christianity was not something I felt that they would approve of. There was a specific passage in Matthew 19 which bothered me a great deal. It was that God had to be first, before family, before everything.

I refused to read it and flatly refused to either understand or accept Rob's explanation. He then gave me a paperback, *I Dared to Call Him Father* by Bilquis Sheikh, which contained an account of a Muslim lady's amazing discovery of God and the troubles and tribulations she had to overcome.[8] This helped put things more in perspective than I thought it would. If someone was willing to die for their faith by proclaiming it, it seemed almost petty for me to worry about how my parents would react. Still, worry I did because after all, I was planning to ask my Buddhist parents to understand enough to allow me to explore this new world I had stumbled upon. Wasn't I just trying to improve my knowledge? It wasn't like I was going to convert.'

Attitude Change

'I remember very well the day that I knew that something in my perception, something in my attitude had changed. That was the day Christianity stopped being a non-threatening concept, and I stopped being an interested, but *uninvolved*, observer. I was talking over lunch with Rob when it hit me that I was actually agreeing with some of the things he was saying. This was getting to be more, much more, than mere curiosity, and I was getting too involved. I decided then and there (though I didn't say anything out aloud) that I had to stop reading any more of the Bible. I thought it was high time I made one of my rare visits to the temple and reaffirm my faith in Buddhism. On my way home from work that day I decided to collect up all the literature Rob had passed on to me, including the Bible, and the next day I would give it all back to him. That was my intention. What actually happened was that I ended up reading and finishing Luke's Gospel. That night I realized that from that moment on, turning my back to God's word wasn't going to be easy.'

She was determined to disprove God through scientific means.

It's perhaps hard for us to understand the turmoil Chandrika was struggling with. The guilt she felt every time she opened the Bible was overwhelming. To assuage this, she was determined, on one level, to disprove God through scientific means. With this in mind, and with enormous difficulty, she obtained membership at the British Museum Library. 'I made extensive notes studying Darwin's theories and concepts put forward by Stephen Hawkins etc. I liked most of the ideas but each night I would come home and read a little more of the Bible, which I felt negated all my hard work during the day. I was very frustrated . . . with myself . . . a person who thus far had been strong-minded – for my apparent inability to stop reading the Bible. My amazement (and my annoyance) came from my easy acceptance of all I read, and my almost over-eagerness to believe. This was not normal for me. I usually analysed and questioned everything, and very rarely accepted anything that conflicted with my preconceived ideas at face value. And yet, here I was, almost tripping over in eagerness to accept and absorb everything in the Bible.'

The morning she finished reading Luke's Gospel found her waking up feeling confused and scared. She had many friends whom she could confide in with all her feelings, but somehow she didn't want to. It was coming up to Christmas and Chandrika got it into her head that she wanted to go to church on Christmas Eve. She invited a very distant relative to accompany her, but he didn't seem particularly keen on the prospect. She had the feeling that he didn't relish the idea of having to explain this particular event to Chandrika's mother when she returned from Sri Lanka. She decided not to push him but, when she happened to mention to Rob at work her desire to go to church, Rob offered to take her. 'I felt very nervous and out of place, until the first carol was sung. The service was short but it touched me quite deeply.'

Soon the holidays were over. Everything was back to normal except that deep in Chandrika's heart was the realization that she had to tell her parents what she was discovering in the Bible. 'All I wanted was that they be patient and understanding with me while I explored this new, intriguing world. Rob and Ananya (another Christian friend) were praying for me, which gave me some much-needed courage to get through. My mother was due back soon. Eventually, after putting off the moment for as long as I could, I went home and found mum had already arrived. I told my mother that I had been to church that morning (not the most subtle of openers), and then proceeded to tell her why. It was at this point that perhaps the most miraculous thing I have ever experienced occurred. Recall my carefully prepared little speech, with just the right, harmless-sounding words etc . . . well, it never took place. From the time I opened my mouth, words gushed from me, proclaiming the depth and magnitude of my belief in Christianity and, more importantly, my public acknowledgement that Jesus Christ was my Lord and Saviour. I have no idea who was more stunned – her or me! This was certainly not even remotely related to what I had planned to say. I sank back in a chair and waited for a response. Finally, gathering herself together, she said, in effect, to do whatever I wanted, and after asking a couple of questions, changed the topic. I was shocked but also greatly relieved. Perhaps it wasn't going to be too difficult?'

But a couple of days later, one of her mum's friends came over. Chandrika had a great deal of respect for this lady and generally cared for her opinion. But it soon became clear that she was not on a social visit. Rather it was out of a concern to clear Chandrika's head of 'these foolish ideas'.

'Though the episode was hurtful at the time, as it involved people I deeply cared for, it left me with two strong convictions. First, I found that I had enough faith in the Lord to know that He would help me keep my stand and give me guidance when the going got tough. Second, I knew that I was finally a Christian where it mattered most . . . in my heart.'

CHAPTER SIXTEEN

Finding Faith

'What is faith?' 'I wish I had your faith!' 'I need more faith.' These are some of the sentiments people often share with me. Maybe you are exploring or still just looking at the aspect of faith . . . or maybe right now you want to get the whole thing sorted.

Some years ago I was helping out with a children's holiday week by the sea. One day, I overheard one of the older team members explaining to a holidaymaker what it meant to become a real Christian. I have never forgotten the clear and helpful way he went through a well-known Bible story drawing from it the steps one must take to get right with God.

First, he turned to the Gospel of Luke (23:39–43) and read the story of the two criminals who were crucified on either side of Jesus when he was on the cross.

One of the criminals who hung there hurled insults at him: 'Aren't you the Christ? Save yourself and us!'

> But the other criminal rebuked him. 'Don't you fear God,' he said, 'since you are under the same sentence? We are punished justly, for we are getting what our deeds deserve. But this man has done nothing wrong.'
>
> Then he said, 'Jesus, remember me when you come into your kingdom.'
>
> Jesus answered him, 'I tell you the truth, today you will be with me in paradise.'

From this we see the steps that the thief, two thousand years ago, and we today, must take to know that our sins are forgiven, so that we can be certain of God and heaven when we die. Having seen in the previous chapters how Jesus really can change lives, it is important that we each know that we have trusted Him to be our personal Lord, Saviour and forever Friend. The thief did not deserve heaven – but then no one does. We have all sinned, and God who is pure, clean and spotless, cannot allow the contamination of wrong into His holy presence. Heaven is filled with sinful people . . . who have been forgiven! First of all, the thief thought of God. He asked his friend, crucified yards away from him, 'Do you not even fear God . . . ?' It may have been the blasphemy of his companion in crime that put the thought of God in his mind. Or perhaps it was the closeness of death, knowing that after death he would meet God and be judged, that made his thoughts turn to God. Sometimes sickness, bereavement, walking away from an accident we shouldn't have survived, or just wanting to thank someone for the beauty of life and the world around, can turn our thoughts to God. Whatever the reason, it is good to consider our Maker, and the one who will, one day, be acknowledged by all as Lord and God. God has revealed Himself to us.

In the Bible, God's written Word, and through the person Jesus Christ, we see that God is eternal, with no beginning or end. He is a spirit. He knows all things, can do all things, and is everywhere. He never changes, and is absolutely reliable and consistent. God is impeccably holy, absolutely just and eternally loving. There is one God, who is three persons: He is Father, Son and Holy Spirit. Repeatedly God had spoken through his prophets that there would come a moment when he would come into the world. Writing seven hundred years before Jesus was born, Isaiah the prophet had said of Jesus:

> For to us a child is born, to us a son is given, and the government will be on his shoulders. And he will be called Wonderful, Counsellor, Mighty God, Everlasting Father, Prince of Peace. Of the increase of His government and peace there will be no end . . .(Is. 9:6)

How much the dying thief understood about God, we don't know, but he was certainly aware that God is Almighty God, and therefore to be feared, and treated with respect.

Then, *the thief thought of his sin*. He shouted across to the thief on the other side of Jesus

> 'Don't you fear God,' he said, 'since you are under the same sentence? We are punished justly, for we are getting what our deeds deserve.'

His crimes were serious. He said that they deserved capital punishment. But no matter how respectable or religious we are, all are guilty of sin against an absolutely holy God. He has given us the Ten Commandments, which are an expression of God's true character. They show us what is right, and that we are wrong. They reveal us to be people who falter and fail. Our sin separates us from God, and would condemn us forever.

We need to be forgiven. It has been a common theme in the preceding chapters. Forgiveness does not come cheaply, nor by turning over a new leaf. It is obtained by receiving it as a free gift from God. Just as a patient needs to be aware how sick he or she really is so that they might go to a doctor to try to find a remedy, we all need to realize how serious our sin is, so that we might go to Jesus, the 'Friend of sinners', for the remedy.

Then, *the dying thief thought of Jesus*. Still shouting across Jesus to his friend on the other cross, the thief said, 'but this man has done nothing wrong.' Quite how he knew this about Jesus, we don't know. Perhaps he knew of a blind man who had been healed by Jesus, or had met a leper cured of his leprosy; perhaps he had been in the crowd when Jesus had taught and then fed the thousands with just a few loaves and fish. Maybe it was the way Jesus had responded when being crucified; his love for his enemies which led Jesus to pray for his executioners that had impressed the thief. Whatever it was, the thief was right. Jesus did no wrong at all. He was the pure, sinless, undefiled Son of God. He was God manifested in the flesh. God became a man and lived here on earth. He came to be the Saviour.

Hanging on the cross, Jesus took on Himself the sin of the world, so that Jesus died paying the penalty of the wrong of which each one of us is guilty. He loved us and gave Himself for us. Carrying on Himself our sin, He provided the means so that all that cuts us off from God could be removed, and we in turn can be reconciled to God.

In thinking of Jesus, the thief was focusing on the only person in the entire world who could help him. He was perhaps hours away from death. Roman soldiers were all around him to make sure there was no escape, except by death. Yet hanging between him and the other thief was the Saviour, sent by God the Father, not to call the righteous, but sinners to repentance. The thief believed in God, was aware of his sin, and was thinking of Jesus, but he was still destined for hell. There had to be the fourth, final, decisive step, which would take him over the line from being an unbeliever in Jesus to someone who was made right with God through Jesus. Then, *he put his trust in Jesus*. We read that

> He said, 'Jesus, remember me when you come into your kingdom.'
> Jesus answered him, 'I tell you the truth, today you will be with me in paradise.'

He didn't offer Jesus any money: they were dying, and the thief's money was probably stolen anyway. He didn't promise to be good or godly from then on: he only had a short time to live. All he could do was cast himself on the mercy of Jesus. That is all God wants us to do. Jesus was carrying the sin of that thief . . . and our sin too. He wants us to receive what He wants to give us. Jesus has the keys to death and hell, and can take a person through life, death and into eternity with him. We simply need to ask Him for pardon and His presence with us. He willingly gives Himself to us. The thief wasn't aware that Jesus would take him to paradise, and would also raise Himself back to life. Jesus won the victory over sin and death.

Today, if we recognize God, and our sin, we too can ask Jesus to forgive us, and to make us His. He will prove Himself to be a wonderful Lord, Saviour, Friend and Companion. On the following page is a prayer you might like to make your own, between you and God.

A Prayer

Dear God,
I am sorry for the things I have done wrong, for my wrong thoughts, and for living without you. I believe Jesus died on the cross for me and took away my sins. I believe that He rose again from the dead. Please forgive me, take control of my life and, with the help of Your Holy Spirit, give me strength to live for you every day.
  In the Name of Jesus,
  Amen

If you would like a copy of John's Gospel and/or further help in confidence, please contact:

D. J. Carswell
c/o Spring Cottage,
Spring Road
Leeds
LS16 1AD
England
Email: carswell77@aol.com

Further Reading

Real Lives, D. J. Carswell (Carlisle: Paternoster, 2001)

Uncovered, Jonathan Carswell (Milton Keynes: Authentic, 2005)

Why Believe?, Roger Carswell (Carlisle: Authentic, 1993)

Why Me?, Roger Carswell (Carlisle: Authentic, 1993)

Uncovering the World, Jonathan Carswell (Milton Keynes: Authentic, 2006)

Where Is God in a Messed Up World?, Roger Carswell (Nottingham: IVP, 2006)

Christianity Explored, Rico Tice and Barry Cooper (New Malden: The Good Book Company, 2002)

Mere Christianity, C.S. Lewis (London: Fount/HarperCollins, 1952)

The Case for Christ, Lee Strobel (Grand Rapids: Zondervan, 1998)

Turning Points, Vaughan Roberts (Carlisle: Authentic, 1999)

References

1 Helpful websites:
www.rainbows.eazytiger.net
www.whenyouwishuponastar.org.uk
www.pasic.org.uk
www.teenagecancertrust.org

2 Millie Murray, with Arthur White, Steve Johnson and Ian McDowall, *Tough Talk* (Carlisle: Authentic, 2000).

3 Further reading: Patrick Sookhdeo, *A Christian's Pocket Guide to Islam* (Fearn: Christian Focus, 2006); Malcolm Steer, *A Muslim's Pocket Guide to Christianity* (Fearn: Christian Focus, 2005).

4 C.S. Lewis, *Mere Christianity* (London: Fount/HarperCollins, 1952).

5 Extract by permission from Emma Carswell, *Love in a Box* (Carlisle: Paternoster, 2001).

6 John Stott, *Basic Christianity* (Grand Rapids: Eerdmans, 1959).

7 www.lmf.org.uk

8 Bilquis Sheikh, with Richard H. Schneider, *I Dared to Call Him Father* (Grand Rapids: Chosen/Baker, 1978).